DYLAN
Redeemed

FROM HIGHWAY 61 TO SAVED

Stephen H. Webb

continuum

NEW YORK • LONDON

The Continuum International Publishing Group, 80 Maiden Lane, New York, NY 10038

The Continuum International Publishing Group Ltd, The Tower Building, 11 York Road, London SE1 7NX

Unless otherwise indicated, biblical quotations are from the New Revised Standard Version Bible, copyright 1989, Division of Christian Education of the National Council of the Churches of Christ in the United States of America. Used by permission. All rights reserved.

Cover art: Getty Images

Cover design: Wesley Hoke

Library of Congress Cataloging-in-Publication Data

Webb, Stephen H., 1961–
  Dylan redeemed : from highway 61 to saved / Stephen H. Webb.
     p. cm.
  Includes bibliographical references (p.   ) and index.
  ISBN-13: 978-0-8264-2755-7 (hardcover)
  ISBN-10: 0-8264-2755-3 (hardcover)
  ISBN-13: 978-0-8264-1919-4 (pbk.)
  ISBN-10: 0-8264-1919-4 (pbk.)
1. Dylan, Bob, 1941—-Religion. 2. Singers—United States—
Biography. 3. Rock music—Religious aspects. I. Title.

  ML420.D98W42 2006
  782.42164092—dc22
  [B]

                                    2006022074

Printed in the United States of America

06 07 08 09 10 11   10 9 8 7 6 5 4 3 2 1

DYLAN
Redeemed

"Hear, a noise! Listen, it is coming—"

—JEREMIAH 10:22

⌒

"yes it is I
who is pounding at your door
if it is you inside
who hears the noise"

—BOB DYLAN, "11 OUTLINED EPITAPHS," LINER NOTES FOR
THE TIMES THEY ARE A-CHANGIN' (1964)

⌒

"So don't fear if you hear
A foreign sound to your ear"

—BOB DYLAN, "IT'S ALRIGHT MA
(I'M ONLY BLEEDING)" (1965)

⌒

Contents

Acknowledgments

hanks to Rodney Clapp for initial encouragement and midway scrutiny, Henry Carrigan for the right amount of patience, Jeff Gordinier for a memorable portrait of my freshman writing teaching routine, and my student, Campbell Robbins, for sharing, among other things, his Johnny Cash collection with me. A bunch of Wabash students have talked to me about my book, but they know how easily I forget names! I can't forget all the help from my research assistant, Joe Seger. I am also very grateful to Jeff Rosen for permission to quote from Bob Dylan's lyrics, and for going the extra mile in letting me use all of the words to the song, "Lay Down Your Weary Tune." And I need to thank to my family for putting up with "all Bob, all the time" at our house. Asher is the exception to the rule that you can't dance to Dylan tunes. This book is for the Friday night boys: Mark Brouwer, J. D. Phillips, Paul Leplae, Patrick Myers, David Kubiak, Will Turner, Jon Baer, Steve Marcou, and David Blix. We've been down in the flood, but it's still all right.

Hearing Dylan in the History of Sound

Alan Lomax (1915–2002) was a missionary for music-ology. He roamed America's backlands in the 1930s recording the forgotten sounds of cowboys, convicts, hobos, and cotton pickers. Convinced that the music of margin-alized people typically took the form of social protest, his research laid the foundation for the folk revival of the late fifties and early sixties. Lomax was a guardian of folk purity, eager to instruct the younger generation in the fine points of musical authenticity. He knew what he liked and why he liked it, and he did not like rock and roll.

Lomax was marshaling all of his hard-earned cultural authority during the Newport Folk Festival in the summer of 1965. His goal was to keep folk music focused on a radical polit-ical message by conserving that music's most traditional forms. Lomax did not think kindly of middle-class white boys trying to pass as black bluesmen, which is what he thought of the Paul

Butterfield Blues Band. On July 25, 1965, he gave them a sneering introduction at a blues workshop, drawing attention to their industrial hardware as evidence of their lack of authenticity. Lomax idealized music that could be played under a tree in the middle of a cotton field, even though many southern black musicians who migrated to Chicago had taken to the electric guitar with all the enthusiasm of people who knew what it was like to live in shacks without electricity. Like many people of his generation, Lomax felt uncomfortable when the excitement of black music jumped the racial line and threatened to shake up white teenagers with sexual energy. When Lomax left the stage, he was challenged by Bob Dylan's manager, Albert Grossman, and the two got into a fight. Dylan was deeply immersed in black musical culture, and he decided to make a stand.

Or perhaps Dylan just wanted to be annoying, since he was in a rocking mood—he came on stage later that evening in a black leather jacket—that did not conform to the laid-back Newport scene. Folk music was not supposed to be flashy. It was not supposed to be original, either. The folk community equated authenticity with a faithful reproduction of the past, while rock and roll was nothing if not a messy blurring of cultural boundaries. Social customs embedded in the legal system prevented blacks and whites from mixing socially, but rock let them mix musically. Middle-class whites learned how to play rock by impersonating black musicians. Dylan stood in favor of musical integration over ideological purity. His ability to absorb nearly any musical style has always been one of his greatest strengths. Dylan was ready to break out of the folk ghetto.

America too was ready for a new sound, but it was not clear that night what the new sound would be or who would sing it. In retrospect, the triumph of rock seems inevitable, but in 1965, rock was still in its infancy. The two years Elvis Presley spent in the army, beginning in 1958, took the steam out of his streak of number one hits, and he was steered into a series of second-rate movies. The Beatles had invaded America in February 1964, mesmerizing female teenagers, but their songs, at first, were more affable than deep. Not until their legendary meeting with Dylan in August 1964 at New York's Delmonico Hotel did their music take a more complex and experimental turn. Dylan and the Beatles pushed each other musically throughout the sixties, but on that day at Newport, Dylan still shared with the folk audience a certain disdain for rock and roll—or at least what rock and roll had become. After its early heyday of sonic brilliance, rock had deteriorated into upbeat tunes about teen love. Few performers even wrote their own songs. As Dylan later explained,

> The thing about rock 'n' roll is that for me anyway it wasn't enough. *Tutti Frutti* and *Blue Suede Shoes* were great catch phrases and driving pulse rhythms and you could get high on the energy but they weren't serious or didn't reflect life in a realistic way. I knew that when I got into folk music, it was more of a serious type of thing. The songs are filled with more despair, more sadness, more triumph, more faith in the supernatural. . . .[1]

The trivia question of who invented rock and roll—Bill Harley, Fats Domino, Little Richard, or Chuck Berry—can still cause endless debates, but there is no question that Bob Dylan reinvented rock that night in Newport. The sunny days of the folk revival were about to be rained out by the thunder of electric guitars and the lightning of pounding drums.

Whatever happened that night—and there are different versions of a stormy performance that has achieved the status of myth—everyone agrees on one thing. Dylan was loud. Dylan might have been angry with Alan Lomax, but he took it out on the audience. When he hit the first note of "Maggie's Farm," many in the audience felt like running for cover. As Joe Boyd, the production manager, remembers, "By today's standards it's not very loud, but by those standards of the day it was the loudest thing that anybody had ever heard."[2] People were literally taken aback. *Tutti Frutti* was smashed to pieces.

Much of the crowd responded by roaring its disapproval back at the band, but that just added to the general confusion. Some people cheered, although firsthand accounts differ on how many. Lomax panicked and wondered who was controlling the sound. That was a prescient question. He and the other organizers sent Boyd to pull the plug, but the thick tangle of listeners prevented him from making it to the soundboard in time. Later an apocryphal story circulated that Lomax or maybe Pete Seeger had tried to cut the sound cable with an ax. While not true, the tale provides a fitting image for the end of one musical period and the beginning of another.

Dylan's detonation was more than just a prank. True, the crowd was smug and casual, full of privileged young people who thought they could change the world just by listening to songs about the down-and-out. Dylan was not above lobbing a sonic bomb into this musical playground of college kids just to get a reaction. His performance, however, was more than just performance art. The folk community had been adroit at using music to stage the drama of leftist ideology. Far from embracing music for its own sake, Dylan was putting on his own counterpolitical theater. His loudness was an aggressive contradiction of the pacifism of the folk crowd, just as his poetic lyrics were a rejection of the folk revival's insistence that songs should be as clear as their political message.[3]

Dylan would later come to regret that his experiment in hyper-sound led so many people to abandon traditional, acoustical music. As has happened so often in his career, his personal journey became programmatic for his generation. As Thomas Hine put it in his book on the making of American teenagers, "Aggressive subjectivity has always been a strain of American culture, of course, but Dylan was the one who made it almost disreputable for a performer simply to sing a song."[4]

Whether he intended to or not, Dylan had broken the musical equivalent of the sound barrier, setting up a noise race that has not ended to this day. Rock seems like second nature today, but those who first heard its earsplitting discordance should be forgiven for thinking it quite unnatural. Dylan had to teach his audience how to hear sounds that had never been heard before. His voice—grating rather than ingratiating—dared you to like it, and the volume at which he played made distortion an integral part of the effect. Some people could never get used to it. Others acted like the music had healed their deafness and that their ears were opened for the very first time.

As these descriptions of Dylan's music suggest, many people describe the awesome power of rock with vocabulary drawn from religious experience. Rock and roll, sex, and drugs are the primary stimulants of modern ecstasy. They promise a momentary pleasure that comes with the dissolution of the isolated, lonely individual. Often combined in an intoxicating brew, rock, sex, and drugs plunge the adolescent self, teetering on the brink of adulthood, into the abyss of excess. Rock and roll is sacred music precisely because it provides a modern analogue to medieval mystical passions.

Rock and religion have become so intertwined in contemporary culture that it is hard to tell them apart. Does rock gain its power from the decline of religious authority, filling in the cultural vacuum created by secularization? Is rock a neutral medium that churches can appropriate with little or no danger to spiritual truths? Do rock and religion both have the same ancient roots, diverging only in the form they give to ecstatic expression? Or is rock essentially at odds with Christianity because of its excitation of sexual desire and its stripping of moral boundaries? That last question might seem prudish, since rock has been domesticated by the aging of the baby boomers, but it is worth remembering how rock concerts once functioned as a kind of pagan rite of passage for many teenagers, immersing them in a cauldron of collective misbehavior.

No contemporary musical artist presents a better test case for examining these questions than Bob Dylan. This is especially true because Dylan is the source of not one but at least two musical revolutions. He provided a bridge between the golden age of rock in the fifties and its reemergence in the sixties by giving folk music an electric jolt. But he also played a key role in the fusion of rock and religion when he converted to Christianity in late 1978. That first revolution made rock harder, faster, and more sophisticated. The consequences of the second revolution, for both music and the church, remain to be seen.

Was it luck, good business sense, or Providence that brought Dylan to the gospel just as gospel music was starting to rock? To answer this question, one needs to know something about the historical context of Dylan's conversion. Dylan turned to Christianity at a critical time in American history, when the liberal Protestant consensus established by the American elite was falling apart and the subsequent cultural vacuum gave evangelical Christians a golden opportunity to take center stage. Prior to the seventies, a liberal Protestant ethos functioned as America's national religion. As President Dwight Eisenhower said, "Our government makes no sense unless it is founded on a deeply held religious belief, and I don't care what it is." The Cold War against the Soviet Union was a battle of ideas, most gravely between Christian freedom and Communist oppression. American citizens could enlist in the conflict by going to church on Sundays. Faith was a civic duty, but it was also incumbent upon all Christians to refrain from being too enthusiastic about their faith. America had to represent reason and restraint in the era of Marxist ideology and Russian intransigence.

By the seventies, this period of socially enforced religious normalcy was coming to an end. Religious passions were not being met in the mainline Protestant churches. Conservative evangelical churches were undergoing rapid growth. Because evangelical Christianity had less of a stake in upholding the social order of the status quo, these churches could be more aggressive in their use of popular culture and technological innovations. The opportunity was wide open for evangelicals to team up with rock and roll in order to reinvent Sunday morning worship. When Dylan became a Christian, he was either riding a new wave of social transformation or helping to direct the storm. Either way, he was once again—just as he was at Newport—in the middle of the musical action.

Dylan's religious period is the focus of this book, but that period cannot be understood apart from a rereading of his entire career. Indeed, it is my argument that a proper understanding of his religious music will necessarily lead to a radical reevaluation of his early career as well, because the usual interpretations of his earlier music stand in the way of an appropriate appreciation of his Christian albums. Far from being merely a blip on his sales charts—or a phase, as if it were a mood he could snap out of—Dylan's Christian period was not an unlikely development in his musical and spiritual journey. It looks unnatural only to those who let a leftist political perspective dominate their interpretations of his work.

Dylan was ahead of the contemporary Christian music trend, since he helped legitimize Christian rock in the late seventies, but even his early music had deeply spiritual undertones. From the beginning of his career, Dylan has talked about his music in terms of a spiritual calling, and scholars like Michael J. Gilmour have documented the way his lyrics, long before his conversion, frequently echo (or quote) the Bible.[5] Dylan has written many classic love songs, but his songs are often preoccupied with love of a higher order. He rose to fame so quickly because he imbued rock with something oracular and otherworldly—a supersonic rendition of the supernatural—which gave popular music enough weight to convey something of the mystery of religious faith. His conversion to Christianity cost him many fans, but they should not have been surprised. He has always taken what seems like a perverse pleasure in frustrating audience expectations.

Nevertheless, few critics are attuned to the theological coherence of Dylan's musical vision. When *Chronicles, Volume One*, the first volume of his autobiography, was published in 2004, reviewers were shocked. Dylan wrote about his life as if he were completely out of sync with the times in which he lived. Fans who were accustomed to the experimental quality of his lyrics, and those few who had read his eccentric book *Tarantula* (1971), an experimental prose poem that is fragmentary and dreamlike, were expecting his autobiography to be postmodern in style, or at least ironic in tone. Instead, they got a printed voice that sounds every bit as authentic as his musical voice. The narrative voice of *Chronicles* is so subdued, generous, and modest that some reviewers thought he was putting on an act. Whatever his faults in his private life, Dylan on stage as well as on the page exudes an unpredictable but essentially honest persona.

Dylan's autobiography has little of the righteous anger that characterizes some of his best songs (except for anger directed at overzealous fans who wanted him to be something he is not). Instead, it demonstrates an apparently endless sympathy for every possible style of American music and a frank tenderness for the perplexities of the human condition. Tagged early in his development with the label of a protest singer, which he never accepted, Dylan could certainly sling snarls from the gutsy regions of his voice. Reading *Chronicles*, however, reveals how deeply Dylan's genius lies in his storyteller's ability to discern other peoples' inner lives.

Chronicles is a dissident history of the sixties—a countercultural response to the counterculture. It could also be described as a study of the cultural currents that lay beneath the underground, since the events Dylan describes have little to do with hippies and the peace movement. Dylan became the voice of his generation by plugging into music that was already decades old by the time the sixties began. Dylan was committed to radical sounds, not radical politics. He was protesting, but his protests were directed against the wickedness of the age, and his musical musings had nothing to do with the idealized socialism and the sexual nihilism that inspired so many of his contemporaries. He breathed life into traditional American music without sacrificing its truth to the deadly demand of political correctness. Fans often obsess over various aspects of Dylan's life—why he sometimes did not give his best in the studio, how he managed to pull off so many comebacks, who influenced him, and who he really is. What puzzles me is how such a unique aesthetic accomplishment could have become interpreted as an expression of the leftist political agenda.

There is something to be learned about anybody by changing the background against which we are accustomed to viewing him or her. What if Dylan in the sixties and afterward was singing against not only social injustice but also against the solutions to social injustice proposed by the political left? I play out that thought experiment in chapter two. Leftist politics has not been kind to, or all that interested in, traditional Christian faith, so this changing of the guard is a prerequisite for a proper analysis of Dylan's Christian period. More than that, once the leftist framework is abandoned, new perspectives on Dylan's entire career emerge.

No Dylan enthusiast has analyzed his work from a theologically and politically conservative perspective. Andrew Gamble comes close with this remark: "Dylan's political message is one of resignation but not of conservativism."[6] What Gamble misses is that resignation in the sixties was the form that conservatism took. Conservatives were down in the flood in the sixties, holding their breaths. In an era that demanded radical change, those who believed in the constancies of human nature and the eternal truths enshrined in the past had to hold their tongues. Passivity with regard to the counterculture spoke for itself. My hunch is that Dylan had conservative political instincts long before the rise of an intellectually credible conservative movement in America. He was conservative before neoconservatives made conservativism cool. Whether such a perspective fits can be judged only by the insights it produces.

Of course, the labels of right and left, liberal and conservative, can be limited and stifling. In the sixties and early seventies, the two major parties were not nearly as homogeneous as they are today. The Democrats had their populist wing in the South, and the Republicans had their libertarian wing in the Northeast. Nixon, for example, rejected the Goldwater wing of his party and worked to gather up the middle of America that Democrats, increasingly influenced by cultural revolutionaries, were abandoning. In the midst of this political tumult, Dylan resisted political labels, so it might seem brazenly inappropriate to put him in yet another box, no matter how newly and neatly constructed. Nonetheless, terms like right and left would not be used so frequently if they did not have a fairly specific and useful range of reference. For better or worse, the American political spectrum is laid out like a shallow, rocky creek with steep, slick banks on the left and the right. Of course, once you begin sliding down one side or the other, things get awfully muddy in the middle.

There are people who try to keep their distance from politics in America, and Dylan is one of them. Politicized readings of Dylan sometimes concede this point by portraying him as a *reluctant* man of the left. He has been quoted as saying that he is not a political person, but staying out of politics is especially hard for a public figure with something to say. Dylan's music is a raging current, so it is understandable that observers feel the need to stand atop the bank on either side to get a good, safe view. Most books about Dylan are written by people who grew up with his music in the sixties, so they reflect the pressures of that period for the dismantling of hierarchies of traditional authority and a loosening of personal moral standards. Dylan both enthralled and frustrated that generation's expectations, which has led to endless cries of betrayal and treachery. Perhaps it is time to view Dylan from a different perspective.

I have no intention of putting Dylan in a political box too small to hold him, or of pushing my own agenda in his name. Yet I am enough of a postmodernist to realize that no interpretation of a great artist is undertaken in a political vacuum. That is why I begin this book, in chapter one, with some autobiographical reflections on growing up as an evangelical Christian in the seventies. My background certainly shapes my reading of Dylan but, more importantly, understanding the battles between religion and popular culture in the seventies is crucial for *any* interpretation of Dylan's conversion at the end of that decade.

Once Dylan is rescued from the political and social radicalism of the sixties, it is much easier to make sense of his Christian convictions, which continue to baffle and dismay many of his most ardent fans. It also becomes much easier to probe the religious depths that reach to the very beginning of his songwriting. During the sixties, Dylan resisted the label of prophet, which the secular press wanted to attach to him, but that does not mean that he was not aware of his religious significance. Even in the sixties, Dylan was more of a religious than a political artist. He has often been called a philosopher and a poet, but I think he is best understood as a musical theologian. He seeks to speak to the heart by converting the ear. I make the case for Dylan as a theologian in chapter three.

Though he resisted the label, Dylan is, in many ways, a modern-day prophet, crying out against the times as Isaiah did in the Old Testament. This is a congenial comparison for many of his fans, because most people today think of the prophets of Israel as the ancient Jewish equivalent of left-leaning liberals today. According to this view, the prophets administered a moral message not too dissimilar from political liberalism's agenda of implementing social justice by overthrowing the burdens of out-dated religious traditions. This is a woefully inadequate under-standing of the prophets, but it also does not do justice to Dylan. His message is disturbing rather than consoling to liberal values. To coin a term, he practices a theo-acoustics that appropriates the biblical tradition of prophecy in a noisy new key.[7] Perhaps by learning to listen to Dylan anew, we can begin to hear the Hebrew prophets in a new way as well.

Contemporary society is saturated in organized sound, so it should be no surprise that theology has morphed into melodic shape. Music is America's most sensuous cultural production, and Dylan, I will argue, is the most powerful of our musical theolo-gians. Most Dylan fans will not take this claim seriously for the understandable reason that they know little or nothing about Christian theology. This is not their fault. Christian theology, like most things associated with religious authority and moral tradi-tion, went into decline in the sixties. The language of sin, salva-tion, and the coming end of the world, which was still the linguistic milieu when Dylan was growing up, had become a for-eign tongue by the time Dylan became a legend. The elite of any culture usually exercise the power of regulating the public expression of religion, but in the sixties, America's cultural elite lost touch with traditional belief. Traditional Christianity was per-mitted to run amok, as long as it did not interfere with sophisti-cated artistic or intellectual activity. By the late seventies, as Ronald Reagan was acutely aware, religious faith was ready to reenter the public realm with a vengeance. The conditions were ripe for an angrier, more edgy expression of popular Christianity.

It is one thing to say that Dylan found his voice with his Christian albums, but it is another thing to describe what his voice means.[8] Descriptions of great art are always inadequate, but writing about the human voice is particularly tricky, since the very act of writing supplants the immediacy of the sounded word. I wrote these pages in the quiet of my office, and you are reading these words silently to yourself. Reading is a form of seeing, not hearing, no matter how our eyes are guided by a still, inner voice. We might imagine well-wrought words in terms of a voice, but that voice is in our heads, while the meaning remains on the page. Looking at something demands description, but hearing can be sufficient in itself. That is why it is comparatively easier to write about painting than music. We are accustomed to describing what we see, whereas sound is transitory and vanishes without losing its value. Describing sound is an act of translation that takes some skill. (In *Chronicles, Volume One*, Dylan exercises this skill in eccentric and vivid ways. For example, he says that Dave Von Ronk's voice was like "rusted shrapnel."[9]) The immediacy of the auditory makes it resistant to general terms, while visual objects actually become more real when we fix them with words.

Dylan's voice is especially challenging to put into words. Many people have tried to come up with funky metaphors to describe his trademark whine—in chapter four I will discuss John Updike's jab, a "Voice You Could Scour a Skillet With"— but it is no easy task to analyze with care the complexity of his tone and the surprising delicacy of his range. As if in acknowledgment of the idea that seeing is more language-bound than hearing, Dylan has portrayed his songwriting in terms of painting, which has long been one of his hobbies. Leonard Cohen, another modern-day Jewish minstrel, was the first of several observers to make the helpful suggestion that Dylan is the Picasso of rock and roll.[10] Like Picasso, Dylan is an artist who works according to his own inner law. Also like Picasso, he has outlived most of his contemporaries and baffled his most loyal fans. Picasso began as a fairly traditional painter who ended up breaking the laws of representation and defying the conventions of drawing. Picasso managed to be both popular and provocative because he toyed with artistic tradition rather than rejecting it outright. Dylan plays with time—music's medium—just as

Picasso was the master of reconfiguring space. Dylan's voice occupies multiple levels of temporal progression simultaneously and defies the traditional laws of harmony. His songwriting is all peculiar angles and intuited associations. His songs arrest your ears just as Picasso's paintings resist a simple scanning of the eye. To put it bluntly, saying that Dylan cannot sing is like saying that Picasso did not know how to draw.

Dylan reinvented rock by working against its one-dimensional surface of sound. He was able to build layers of depth into his songs by drawing from musical styles that many middle-class Americans had never heard. Because Dylan's music is firmly rooted in the traditional genres of blues, gospel, Appalachian, and country and western, it has staying power that most rock and roll lacks. His commitment to tradition allows him to be innovative without getting lost in fads and fashions. His music is truly histori-cal, in the sense that he is continually paying his debt to voices from the past. Death, in fact, haunts many of his best lyrics, but you can also hear death in his voice. He sings like one who has been living with the dead for a long time. He can say with Isaiah, "The Lord God has given me the tongue of those who are taught that I may know how to sustain the weary with a word" (50:4). He strives for the new by honoring the old, a strategy of renewal that can be as complex as it is captivating. I try to articulate in written form the religious layers of Dylan's voice in chapter four.

Finally, in chapter five, I return to the question of the nature of rock and roll and its relationship to religion. Things have changed since Dylan first went electric back in 1965, and not just with baby boomers who are now buying hearing aids by the thousands. Rock has been so drummed into our heads that much of it sounds banal and boring. Never before have so many people known so much about music, but music also seems more trivial than ever before. Music is everywhere you go, but the inflationary pressures on music have diminished its value. We hardly register its sonic presence while we eat, drink, drive, and shop. Music was once reserved for religious rituals and social occasions of great gravity. Now our ears are so plugged-in that we are deaf to its magic. We walk around in sound cocoons that block out all the competing noise, as if our lives need a sound-track to be meaningful. Technology gives us the power to listen to what we want when we want it but, as a result, we spend a lot of time listening alone. There are more beats than ever before, but everyone marches to one of his or her own making.

What the baby boomers began in rebellion has ended in the acoustical equivalent of wallpaper. The very term *baby boomer* sounds like it belongs to the era of rock and roll, and it does. Rock was born on the tide of the buying power of all those babies who became teenagers during the sixties. Music, in other words, has been drafted into the service of our consumer soci-ety. Rock either incites us to buy and buy again or anesthetizes us to the anxiety provoked by the countless buying decisions we must constantly make. Rock music has become both the stimu-lant and the sedative of modern capitalism. This underscores Dylan's importance, because it is hard to imagine an advertising agency turning his sound into an audio brand for profitable dis-tribution and quick consumption.

Teenagers are angst-driven to know what is popular and what is not, and rock is the quintessence of popular culture. Rock can be defined as whatever music is most current—it exists on the edge of time in its quest for the newest and latest sounds. In practical terms, rock songs come and go so quickly that only the constant consumer can keep up with the latest trends. Rock also buttresses the teenage fantasy of making it big without undergoing years of tedious training by holding out the seductive promise that becoming a star is as easy as singing along with the radio. Christianity is about the making of saints, not stars. One might become a Christian in an instant, but becoming a saint takes time, and it takes a willingness to stand apart from popular culture. All of these concerns lead to a most pointed question: Can Christianity survive the age of rock and roll?[11]

That question is pressing to me because I grew up in an era when sacred and secular music were enmeshed in a sound war, but my students have grown up in a time when rock and religion have signed a mutual nonaggression pact. My students are so immersed in the music of the moment that Dylan's Christian period is ancient history, if they know it at all. I want to show throughout this book how Dylan stands at the center of debates about the future of rock and roll and the meaning of Christian worship. If Christians do not know how to listen to the way Dylan raised rock to the level of the gospel, how can they expect to be prepared to know when the gospel is being lowered to the level of rock? If Christians are to experience a sense of holiness through music and, at the same time, redeem popular culture from its miasma of meaninglessness, then Christians need to think about Dylan now more than ever before.

Dylan, of course, is a musician on the move, and he surely has more surprises in store for us as his faith ripens along with his voice. For what he has accomplished so far in his life, he can be acclaimed as one of the greatest American theologians of the latter half of the twentieth and the beginning of the twenty-first century. Even those sympathetic to this claim might think that statement a bit hyperbolic. When the fallout of his conversion to Christianity is finally sorted out, however, it might prove to be an understatement. Dylan's conversion constitutes a seismic shift in our sonic culture, and even the Christian community has not fully come to terms with the gospel songs he produced in the late seventies and early eighties. This is unfortunate, because of all the American artists of the last fifty years—popular or elite—he is one of the very few to develop an essentially conservative view of Jesus. This is what continues to baffle his fans and critics. The man they thought would lead the way of the counterculture turns out to be, in their view, altogether anti-culture instead.

Notes

1. Bob Dylan *Biograph* (Columbia, 1985), with liner notes and text by Cameron Crowe, p. 26.

2. Interview with Joe Boyd in *Wanted Man: In Search of Bob Dylan,* ed. John Bauldie (New York: Citadel Press, 1990), p. 64.

3. The best discussion of the musical shape of Dylan's rejection of folk music can be found in the essays in *The Political Art of Bob Dylan*, ed. David Boucher and Gary Browning (New York: Palgrave Macmillan, 2004). Also see Stephen H. Webb, "It Ain't Me Babe," in *First Things* (August/September 2006), 49–54.

4. Thomas Hine, *The Rise and Fall of the American Teenager* (New York: Avon Books, 1999), p. 263.

5. Michael J. Gilmour, *Tangled Up in the Bible: Bob Dylan and Scripture* (New York: Continuum, 2004).

6. Andrew Gamble, "The Drifter's Escape," in *The Political Art of Bob Dylan*, p. 32. Also in this volume see the insightful application of the category of "expressionism" to Dylan in David Boucher, "Images and Distorted Facts: Politics, Poetry and Protest in the Songs of Bob Dylan," pp. 134–69.

7. For more on the concept of theo-acoustics, see Stephen H. Webb, *The Divine Voice: Christian Proclamation and the Theology of Sound* (Grand Rapids: Brazos, 2004).

8. For the most careful analysis of Dylan's voice, see Michael Daley, "Vocal Performance and Speech Intonation: Bob Dylan's 'Like a Rolling Stone,'" in *Bob Dylan Anthology Volume 2: 20 Years of Isis*, ed. Derek Barker (Surrey, England: Chrome Dreams, 2005), pp. 104–15.

9. Bob Dylan, *Chronicles, Volume One* (New York: Simon & Schuster, 2004), p. 262.

10. Bauldie, ed., *Wanted Man: In Search of Bob Dylan*, p. 142.

11. One could also ask: Can rock and roll survive the death of Christianity? Some scholars think we live in a post-Christian culture, where Christianity continues to survive but has less impact on political and cultural issues. The substance of American culture, these scholars argue, is no longer Christian. If this is true, and if rock has risen to prominence as a substitute religion by organizing a counter-Christian process of social formation, what will happen to rock when it has nothing to work against? In other words, if the power of rock and roll depends on its competitive and ambivalent relationship to Christianity, in a purely secular culture, rock just might sound boring.

CHAPTER ONE

Saved from the Seventies

For evangelical Christians in 1979, a born-again Dylan was as electrifying as his 1965 decision to plug in his guitar at the Newport Folk Festival. I graduated from high school in 1979, and I knew next to nothing about the way Dylan had transformed rock by making it sound poetic and had alienated folk audiences by playing loud and hard. But the rumor that Bob Dylan had been saved struck my ears like a thunderbolt from the sky. And when I listened to his first Christian album, *Slow Train Coming* (1979), I heard the gospel proclaimed to my heart in a way that finally made sense to my ears.[1]

In the late seventies, evangelicals like me needed a musical hero who could speak to the disturbing chasm that separated the harmony of Sunday morning from the discord of Saturday night. We wanted a sonic power to match the depths of our experience of salvation, but we also just wanted to listen to rock and roll with a clean conscience. In my midwestern evangelical home, rock and roll was treated like an unwelcome guest who showed up late, loud, and drunk during times of family strife. Inevitably, my dad would have to ask him to leave. Now the greatest rocker of all time was one of us.

I had grown up in the dull days of pre-CCM (Christian Contemporary Music). Back then, conservative churches had conservative music. We thought *that* was what made us conservative—patiently enduring music that was at least two generations behind the times. We sang songs that were not that far removed from the days of barbershop quartets. My folks didn't even listen to Frank Sinatra, although I had an aunt who did. She was a Methodist, a church that was in the middle of the mainstream. Our church was so liturgically low that we were not even part of any official denomination.

Only later did I find out that many of the tunes to our hymns originated in beer halls and taverns. That was surprising, because growing up I was repeatedly told that only evil could come from those kinds of places. Ex-soldiers must have populated those taverns, because most of our hymns sounded like battle marches. Those strident tunes fit our theology just fine. Evangelicals in the seventies were an embattled minority, fighting for survival in a hostile environment. We were spiritual soldiers in training, at war with the world. In Sunday school, we chanted hypnotic lyrics that drummed jingoistic messages into our heads. One song still bounces around in my memories: "We are jet cadets for Jesus, we are pilots for the Lord, we have heard the call for battle and we'll join with one accord. Come and join our happy crew as we soar into the sky. We are jet cadets for Jesus and we'll fly, fly, fly." That was our way, as one Sunday school teacher recommended, of getting high on Jesus.

When our music was not militaristic, it was maudlin. We were either singing in formation like a boot camp battalion or crying our hearts out over the way we treated Jesus. Only later did I realize just how much the maudlin songs had in common with country-and-western music. We sang like unfaithful lovers who had to throw ourselves—"Just as I am, without one plea"—into the arms of our man.

I turned 10 in 1971, so the seventies fit my teen years like the tight pair of purple-and-red plaid bell-bottoms that I proudly wore throughout seventh grade. My older brother was just old enough to pass for a child of the sixties, and I grew up in his shadow. That is probably why I think of the seventies as a kindred spirit, since it too could not compete with its older sibling. Goofy and tacky are two words that come to mind when I try to describe a decade that will always be treated as the kid brother to the sixties. Even the economic crisis of the seventies—stagflation—has none of the dignity of a depression or recession. When John Travolta's character in *Saturday Night Fever* yelled at his father, "Would you just watch the hair," I could relate. Despite the fad for happy face buttons, it was a dreadful decade. It began with fervent idealism on the political left and ended up with the same mood co-opted by Ronald Reagan on the right. In between was a time of lost innocence, cultural confusion, and moral decadence.

The seventies were one long lesson in what happens when a counterculture becomes normalized.[2] When the hip becomes everyday, reality suffers. Hipness works best when it lies on the margin of the mainstream, feeding popular culture with a new vocabulary in order to expand society's vision of what the good life should be. If the margin becomes the mainstream, flooding results. This is just common sense. Social practices that emerge from a radical critique of bourgeois society cannot themselves become the basis of a stable society. If that happens, the radical loses its edge and the bourgeoisie collapse into a moral morass. But that is just what happened in the seventies. The political left suffered a backlash with the election of Nixon and transformed itself into a cultural left. The triumph of the cultural left in many of our most important institutions rendered common sense senseless. The cultural left taught people to mistrust the conformity of social conventions. Everything had to be reinvented, especially anything having to do with sex. Today, when most Americans have returned somewhat to their senses, it's hard to imagine a time when black light posters, beaded curtains, water pipes, and feathered roach clips could be found in gift shops at the local mall. The cooler among us had faux fishing nets hanging from our bedroom ceilings as a sign of authenticity.

If the term *culture* is taken lightly, it can be said that no decade in the twentieth century had more cultural changes than the seventies, and thus no decade is harder to describe. This is true in spite of the fact that most of these cultural changes were exceedingly trivial, because their cumulative effect was profoundly depressing. For example, the seventies gave us the divorce culture, as if those two words are in any way compatible. With skyrocketing divorce rates, the middle-aged began making up for lost time by acting half their age. The establishment adopted the accoutrements of the anti-establishment. Even Jimmy Carter wore jeans and posed as an outsider. It seems silly to portray teenagers as the victims of fashion, but that is what pictures of girls in tube tops and boys with Scott Baio haircuts (blow-dried into "wings") look like today.

The purpose of these bad fashions was to make the sixties safe for suburbia. *The Partridge Family*, for example, made sixties rock and roll a family affair. How many families made up a band with the mother singing along—and with no father around to yell at them to turn it down? *Happy Days* turned the menace of Fonzie, the fifties tough guy, into a joke. *The Brady Bunch* was so sickly sweet and harmlessly vacuous that it can only be understood as the superficial counterpart to the moral decadence that television sitcoms could not yet glorify. There were shows that strained for moral relevance, like *All in the Family*, but the form these shows took was confessional rather than prophetic. The whole point was whether Archie could find some way to rationalize his crude behavior, and whether Mike would find a way of connecting to his father-in-law in spite of his own high-sounding rhetoric. After all, this was the decade when everyone decided to start baring their private lives on TV, with the ever-earnest Phil Donahue leading the way. Gossip was raised to the art of dignified conversation. Endless divulgences of aberrant behavior took the place of moral principles. In an era when mood rings were taken seriously, is it any wonder that people felt lost?

Bad fashion was just the tip of a moral iceberg hollow to the core, and by the middle of the decade, America was blindly heading toward disaster. Just observe how the radical chic style of the sixties had become baroque in the seventies. When a society begins expressing itself by imitating the immediate past, something is missing in the present. The seventies, in fact, were filled to the brim with an empty nostalgia. In our junior high variety show, we dressed up like we were going to a sock hop, with girls in poodle skirts and boys in scoop-neck T-shirts, greased-back hair, and rolled-up jeans. Students today are still nostalgic, of course—they have eighties dances!—but they are more sophisticated about the way the media uses nostalgia to sell everything from soap to sports cars. We were more innocent about the possibility of being transported into the past, though the danger of sophistication is that it can easily slip into cynicism. The seventies were the last time in American history when nostalgia could be innocent, pure, and sweet. When people get nostalgic for the seventies today, they are being nostalgic for our loss of nostalgia.

The bad fashions included the popular music, which was often little more than sentimental melodies of idealized sexual desire. In that respect, the soft rock of the seventies was not that different from the evangelical songs we poured out in church. If we weren't flying high like jet cadets for Jesus, we were singing the theme song to *Gilligan's Island* or asking Ricky not to lose that number. The Monkees were a made-up band with a goofy TV show, and we were their target audience. Already the early Beatles songs were the subject of nostalgia, and their heartfelt harmonies provided a nice blend for families that were trying to move straight from the fifties into the seventies. More threatening music lurked on the horizon. Hard rock was beginning to blast away at the pack of puppy-love songs that crowded top-40 radio. Something strange was happening to sound. Electricity powered a shocking break from the past. Loudspeakers permitted large crowds, and audiences were encouraged to be as loud as the music, which was deafening anyway. Heavy metal was menacing, but it was also more stimulating than much of the soft rock of the day. Given the anxiety of our nation's prolonged retreat from Vietnam, it is understandable that the abrasive became soothing. Evangelicals did not know whether to organize a charge or signal for retreat, but they did draw stark battle lines between the comforts of the church and the increasingly secular ways of the world.

Hard rock got harder. If our ears had had lids, we would have kept them tightly shut. The heaviness of rock was merely one sign of the confusing signals being broadcast by popular culture. I went to my first hard rock concert—a local band that had one radio hit—at about the same time that I visited a friend's Pentecostal church for the first time. Both events overwhelmed my sense of hearing. Churches and concerts were both getting louder. It is hard to understand today just how radical these acoustical changes were. No one knows for sure when rock was born, but it had to be continually reborn to stay alive. With the aging of every cycle of consumers, rock musicians had to inflame deadened nerves anew. Rock was not a style or a statement as much as it was a movement in the purest sense of that word: it *moved*, speeding through the notes, blurring the words, morphing into new forms. This could add up to a lot of excitement, but it could also add up to nothing at all: motion plus energy without any purpose or end.

My father's generation was just a little bit too old to find Elvis exciting. They were too busy building new lives in the suburbs that sprang up all over America after World War II. Suburbanite parents thought of themselves as explorers, tending gardens, building civic organizations, mastering home repair, and planting new churches. They were escaping, in part, from the city noise that could be so distracting and exhausting. People naturally seek the source of the sounds they hear, but city noise is so constant and varied that urbanites must practice selective listening, blocking out anything that does not really matter. Selective listening can be draining. Scholars of the history of sound have pointed out how the bourgeoisie in Victorian England demanded the right to be free from the noise of the lower classes.[3] This same trait marked the middle class in suburban America. The privacy of the suburbs was valued largely because it offered protection from the invasion of unwanted sounds. Ironically, those very same suburbs were the seedbeds of rock and roll. Simply put, teenagers were bored with all the peace and quiet. The dead air smothered their sense of possibilities. Teens turned to rock to make their isolated lives sound a little more urban.

My parents' generation sensed that rock music was divisive by its very nature. As much as I thought then that they added to that divisiveness by their stubborn refusal to listen to the beat, I think now that they were more right than wrong. We lived in a ranch-style house with potato chip–thin walls. Unfortunately, rock music needs to be played loud or it just doesn't sound right. At least that's what I told my parents, who were tone deaf to its appeal. They responded to every antagonistic guitar riff with anger of their own. We compromised by buying a set of headphones.

The headphones were useful in figuring out the words lost in the noise. Even today, there are Web sites devoted to ongoing debates over the correct content of popular lyrics. It should not be surprising, then, that someone got the idea to slow down the spinning turntable to investigate the needle's ride. Since the sixties, people had been fascinated with the idea that advertisers could hide hidden messages in visual images. Now it was music's turn. Rumors began spreading about satanic lyrics pressed into the vinyl grooves of LPs. It was as if Christian leaders reacted to the idea that rock stars were gods by insisting that their music really was full of the devil. Ironically, the idea that evil messages could be discerned in garbled lyrics only made us listen to records all the harder. We turned our attention to the minutiae of rock songs just as we scanned every word of the Bible, hunting for signs meant just for us.

Not every evangelical reaction to rock and roll was so desperate. By the end of the seventies, evangelicals were beginning to come out of their prayer closets. We listened to Phil Keagy, Larry Norman, and Keith Green, who were pioneers in the appropriation of rock for worship and evangelization. Green, a truly brilliant musician with a sound all his own, would become a friend of Dylan before he died in a plane crash in 1982. Green was a Jewish Christian whose lyrics were every bit as uncompromising as Dylan's. We knew Dylan's conversion was for real when we saw his name as a guest artist on the back of Green's *So You Wanna Go Back to Egypt* (1980). My circle of evangelical friends spent hours speculating about such questions as who led Dylan to Christ and how he was going to change the world. We wondered if the hippies were closer in lifestyle to the early Christians than our middle-class neighbors were. We convinced each other that Phil Keagy was a better guitarist than Clapton or Hendrix, and that Larry Norman could have become a major rock star if he had wanted to. We were not alone in our need for a new musical theology. Christian rock was on its way up. It needed just one last boost before it made it over the wall that separated evangelicals from the rest of the world.

Evangelicals like us had one foot in the popular culture with one remaining in our religious ghetto, and it was tearing us apart. We could no more avoid the mass media than we could skip church on Sunday mornings. Conservative Christians were just beginning to build their own culture, but that would take years to get off the ground. When that happened, evangelical teenagers would not feel compelled to choose between the church and the world. They could have all the benefits of a close-knit community and all the fun of the entertainment industry. They did not need to reject the world, because their churches started giving them everything the world had to offer. The first big step in that direction was turning rock and roll into an instrument for the gospel. If the church could capture the music of the devil, then heaven could not be far away.

Dylan has always epitomized the longings of those who seek something salvific from popular music. He has served this function against his will, but his passion for privacy has only magnified his legend, funding a small industry of obsessive fans trying to figure out who he really is. When he converted to Christianity, he broke the cultural mirror that had threatened to imprison his image. His conversion was too much for the popular media to take, and his most loyal fans were at a loss to understand what happened. He was saved, but his fans seemed lost.

Throughout the early eighties and early nineties, Dylan's Christianity was the subject of intense debate. He followed *Slow Train Coming* (1979) with *Saved* (1980) and *Shot of Love* (1981), but soon after this trio of explicitly Christian albums there were rumors about a return to Judaism and nonstop speculation about his religious state of mind. Many fans kept looking for an explicit disavowal of Christian faith, which never came. What was harder for the secular media to understand was that as Dylan matured, so did his theology, but the media has never accepted the fact that religious beliefs can be complex and multifaceted. Soon journalistic inquiries into his religious convictions became more infrequent and finally fell silent altogether—perhaps out of respect for Dylan's own quiescence on the topic. I watched these developments with an increasing sense of wry detachment from the secular world that I was in the process of trying to join, yet I could never get those Christian albums out of my mind—especially the first one, released in 1979, when I was at the peak of my strident evangelicalism.

That year was the peak of Dylan's religious enthusiasm as well. While he was preaching to audiences in San Francisco, I was editing an evangelical newspaper and passing it out to my classmates at high school. Many of them gave me strange looks, but I set my vision on higher things. I can relate to the intensity of Dylan's witness. I can also relate to the way he later toned down his message, maybe even feeling a little bit embarrassed about his born-again enthusiasm. Dylan's music as well as his theology has evolved since then in ways that have been as helpful to me as his more evangelical sound was twenty-five years ago. I listened to his music from the sixties and seventies only after I heard his Christian albums, and I was surprised by what I found. Many of his early songs sounded familiar to my gospel-trained ears, and many of those lyrics seemed to anticipate his conversion.

I became a fan, eagerly awaiting each new album, but it took me years before I was ready to listen to *Slow Train Coming* again. That album took me back to my evangelical youth too quickly and too forcefully. When I finally played it again in the late nineties, it took my breath away and left me gulping for air. It was as if the apostles had come back to life and were putting the day of Pentecost to music. To some the album sounds preachy and pious, but that was not my problem. To me, it sounds painfully honest and true. *Slow Train Coming* convicts my conscience with the sound of a faithful purity that I am too often unable to muster with the same enthusiasm. It sets me dreaming of what I know faith can and should be. That album is and always will be what faith sounds like to me. I could no more turn my back on it than I could turn my back on the faith of my youth. Coming to terms with it meant looking in the mirror of Dylan's music for something more than his enigmatic personality or even my own spiritual journey. It meant looking for the acoustical shape of salvation.

Notes

1. For an amusing fictional portrait of the impact of Dylan's conversion on a group of teenagers on Christian retreat, see the brilliant coming-of-age novel by Marshall Boswell, *Trouble with Girls* (New York: Bantam Dell, 2003), chap. 3.

2. My memory and analysis of the seventies have been stimulated by several fascinating books on that decade, including David Frum, *How We Got Here, The Seventies: The Decade That Brought You Modern Life (For Better or Worse)* (New York: Basic Books, 2000); Shelton Waldrep, ed., *The Seventies: The Age of Glitter in Popular Culture* (New York: Routledge, 2000); Pagan Kennedy, *Platforms: A Microwaved Cultural Chronicle of the 1970s* (New York: St. Martin's Press, 1994); Philip Jenkins, *Decade of Nightmares: The End of the Sixties and the Making of Eighties America* (New York: Oxford University Press, 2006); Andreas Killen, *1973 Nervous Breakdown: Watergate, Warhol, and the Birth of Post-Sixties America* (New York: Bloomsbury, 2006); and Edward D. Berkowitz, *Something Happened: A Political and Cultural Overview of the Seventies* (New York: Columbia University Press, 2006).

3. Peter Bailey, "Breaking the Sound Barrier," in *Hearing History: A Reader*, ed. Mark M. Smith (Athens: University of Georgia Press, 2004), p. 31.

CHAPTER TWO

A Conservative
Out of Time

G. K. Chesterton, the Victorian-era convert to Catholicism and one of the most gifted defenders of the church, observed in a book about the great medieval theologian Thomas Aquinas, "It is the paradox of history that each generation is converted by the saint who contradicts it most."[1] This is a striking statement in any context, but especially when applied to Bob Dylan. Dylan became a superstar not because he was saying what everyone already wanted to hear. Throughout the sixties, there were plenty of gurus telling young people to cut their ties to the past in order to embrace the dawn of the new Age of Aquarius, whatever that meant. Dylan was not one of them. Instead, he was an audible sign of contradiction in the midst of confusing cultural changes. He rarely catered to the tastes of his audience, just as he rarely gave straight answers to media interviews. Dylan's secret, which is only fully revealed in his autobiography, is that he became the conscience of his generation by contradicting it.

That, perhaps, is giving his generation too much credit, because it is not clear what Dylan converted his generation to. It is not too hard to understand that each age needs to be contradicted, but Chesterton's maxim does not explain how people can come to accept a contradiction, let alone be saved by it. Christian saints are able to accomplish this trick because they live by grace, and their lives take the form of that most persuasive contradiction, the cross. Though Dylan, especially in the seventies, could identify himself as a Christ figure, he knew he was no saint. He also suspected that most Americans no longer had the capacity to respond to saints. As he sang in one of his greatest theological works, "I Dreamed I Saw St. Augustine," from *John Wesley Harding* (1968),

> No martyr is among ye now
> Whom you can call your own
> So go on your way accordingly
> But know you're not alone.[2]

In this dream song, Dylan sees St. Augustine searching for souls to no avail. Augustine is preaching "in a voice without restraint," which is a good description of how Dylan sang prior to this album. Dylan recognizes that he is one of those "who put him out to death." The song ends with Dylan terrified and crying, bowing his head and putting his fingers against the glass. Dylan's song takes Chesterton's statement one step further. Chesterton says that the saint we need is inevitably the saint we cannot understand. Dylan says we live in a time without saints altogether—or at least without saints we can recognize. Yet the song leaves us with the hope that the very absence of saints might be enough to remind us of what we are missing.

Dylan kept searching for something transcendent, but his fans froze him in place with their needy gaze. Nobody likes to be contradicted, which is why the sixties tastemakers were so eager to misread Dylan. To take but one example, Nat Hentoff's liner notes for *The Freewheelin' Bob Dylan* (1963) imply that "A Hard Rain's A-Gonna Fall" was written about the Cuban missile crisis, despite the fact that Dylan sang it at Carnegie Hall three weeks before the crisis began. This little bit of leftist political fantasy has entered the Dylan lexicon with the status of a myth because it served the agenda of the Dylan mythmakers.

Social and political radicals have always been trying to make Dylan mirror their political piety. When it became clear that Dylan was not the voice of social justice the left wanted him to be, the media recreated him as a harbinger of anarchy. Dylan has encouraged that tag (he called himself "the Archbishop of Anarchy" in his 2004 *60 Minutes* television interview), even though his abiding concern for truth and morality shows it to be little more than a joke. Given the emergence of deconstruction, postmodernity, and the study of popular culture in university English departments in the late seventies, it was probably inevitable that critics would drop the idea of Dylan as a political radical and instead begin portraying him as a cultivator of irony, hiding behind masks and toying with the vicissitudes of self-identity. From this perspective, Dylan is the Kierkegaard of rock and roll.

In fact, the impossibility of locating Dylan along the spectrum of leftist politics has afflicted Dylanologists with a plague of anxiety. If the personal is political, according to sixties logic, then surely the most personal of modern art forms—music—is, at least potentially, revolutionary. The evidence that rock and roll has been a force for left-leaning social change, however, is slim to none.[3] Sixties intellectuals commended rock for its revolutionary potential, hoping it would overthrow more than just our customary ways of hearing, but in actuality, rock merely functioned to set apart the young as an identifiable consumer group, thus expanding the range of capitalist markets. What revolution rock unleashed was social, not political, as it spread youth culture up (and now, increasingly, down) the ladder of years. Rock has hardly promoted revolutionary views of women, blacks, or the poor. If rock has failed to ignite dramatic social change, then it is all the more important for those who are radically inclined to uphold at least one rock star as a would-be revolutionary. If Dylan, arguably the greatest rocker of them all, was essentially a political spokesman for the left, then even if he betrayed the left, his original political motivation shows how deeply rooted rock is in the progressive cause. If Dylan is not, or was not, a man of the left, and if rock is not the voice of liberalism, then why have so many left-leaning liberals devoted so much time and effort gushing about rock's political thrills?

The resulting anxiety leaves a contradiction at the core of many of the best books about Dylan. Dylanologists tend to make two claims that are incommensurable. They argue that Dylan is a great artist who has put together a body of musical work unparalleled among modern singer-songwriters. I agree. They also argue that Dylan is a master of disguise who sheds his musical skin faster than a pollster can predict the next fashion trend. Thus Larry David Smith, in his massive homage to the man he strikingly calls a "sonic sponge," portrays him as an actor who is able to disappear into the characters he plays.[4] Great artists are as cunning as they are coherent, but the idea that Dylan is both singular in his music and multiple in his personalities just does not make much sense. What drives these confusions is the way Dylan resists being plotted on the typical narrative graph about sixties political radicalism. It is as if liberals, once they become unsure of Dylan's own liberal credentials, are convinced that he must be confused about himself. Or, as an exasperated friend told me when I suggested that Dylan was not a typical liberal, "But what else could he have been?"

Whether he was seen as confirming the political relevance of social rebellion or previewing the liberating possibilities of postmodernism, Dylan was lionized as the great radical of the sixties. He was subsequently demonized as an artistic failure in the seventies and as a Christian sellout in the early eighties. His friends and foes could not wait for signs that he was leaving his faith behind. When Dylan recorded a throwaway tribute to Lenny Bruce on *Shot of Love*, Allen Ginsberg could not have been happier. He took Dylan's sympathy for the outsider comedian as a sign that Dylan's born-again phase was coming to an end. Worse than being a particularly egregious example of wishful thinking, Ginsberg's remark demonstrates his religious prejudice by assuming that a Christian could never have felt compassion toward a drug-addicted comic down on his luck.[5]

A Freudian might propose a simple explanation for the outpouring of anger at Dylan's conversion: it was the unconscious revenge that sixties radicals took on him for not fulfilling their political fantasies. The more Dylan resisted the role he was assigned, the more his most ardent fans wanted him to stick to the script they had written for him. Myth works to protect us against knowledge that hurts, just as love answers a need to be known better than we can know ourselves. Dylan's music speaks knowingly to us, but what he has to say is not pleasant or reassuring. Perhaps it will be several generations before his music seeps so far into the American soul that we will be able to listen to him in a way that he deserves—by loving his music, not his myth.

The sixties were full of mythmakers. The entire decade is lost in the haze of myth. Historians are only recently coming to terms with its political complexity. Campus politics were less polarized and more diverse than most portraits of the sixties depict. There was plenty of confusion, anger, and hope to fuel political passions along the entire range of the political spectrum. Until the Tet Offensive in 1968 began consolidating student opinion against the Vietnam War, protests against Communism were not unusual (often led by members of Young Americans for Freedom), and campus radicals committed to leftist ideology were in a small minority on nearly all American campuses. According to a spring 1968 Gallup poll, only 8 percent of students considered themselves "radical or far left," and only 16 percent agreed with the statement that "the war in Vietnam is pure imperialism," a number that would rise to 41 percent the next year. Campus radicals seemed more prevalent because they turned politics into theater and mastered the skills of self-promotion. Consequently, they received attention out of proportion to their actual numbers. It should also be remembered that it was in the interest of conservatives (at that time and even today) to play up the influence of the more radical elements of the campus left, since their excesses helped end the hegemony of liberalism in America.

Campus radicals pursued careers in higher education at a much higher rate than campus conservatives, so most histories of the sixties are one-sided at best. The twin forces of nostalgia and self-justification have led to a monolithic portrait of a generation that was as politically mixed as it was socially mixed-up. The folk scene that Dylan engaged when he moved to New York in 1961 was certainly on the political left, but Dylan frustrated that crowd musically and only flirted with it politically. Dylan examined the hearts of his contemporaries with the same offbeat eye that scanned record collections for the obscure and the unheard. He read old newspapers from the Civil War period, when the American language was steeped in Christian piety. His favorite politician, he tells us in *Chronicles*, was Barry Goldwater, "who reminded me of Tom Mix, and there wasn't any way to explain that to anybody."[6] In a 1989 interview with Edna Gundersen of *USA Today*, he was asked about the sixties mantra, "Don't trust anyone over thirty." "From '66 on," he responded, "I was trying to raise a family, and that was contrary to the whole epidemic of the '60s. Most people were running away from home and trying to run away from their parents. That was never intentional on my part, trying to run away from anything. My family was more important to me than any kind of generational '60s thing. Still is. To find some meaning in the sixties for me is real far-fetched. . . . The sixties will be forgotten."[7]

In 1967, the so-called summer of love, Dylan was living in Woodstock and, by all reports, spending time each day studying the Bible and the Hank Williams songbook. When Noel Stookey, the Paul of Peter, Paul and Mary, made a pilgrimage to the master, full of flower power and looking for the answers to the meaning of life, Dylan simply asked him, "Do you ever read the Bible?"[8] That year, all the hip bands were trying to match the dense and hallucinogenic sound of the Beatles' *Sgt. Pepper's Lonely Hearts Club Band*. The Beatles had quit touring in 1966 to devote their musical energy to the studio, where they invented unique acoustical combinations that would have been impossible to reproduce on the stage.

Dylan went his own direction. In fact, he went out of his way in 1967 to go to Nashville to record the intensely subdued *John Wesley Harding* (which includes "I Dreamed I Saw St. Augustine"). Most of his fans missed the album's message at the time, but close readers of his lyrics today estimate that it has more than sixty biblical allusions. Rock journalist Stephen Davis compared it to a "new acoustic psalms."[9] Dylan's biographer Anthony Scaduto called it "Dylan's avowal of faith."[10] In a 1976 interview with *TV Guide's* Neil Hickey that preceded his conversion to Christianity by two years, Dylan referred to it as "the first biblical rock album."[11] He could be facetious in that interview, as when he said that his favorite music was sound-effect records.[12] But the seriousness in his words was unmistakable when he told Hickey that the highest form of song is prayer.

John Wesley Harding was released a year before the official birth of Christian rock. Larry Norman's *Upon This Rock* (Capitol, 1969) is widely regarded as the album that first recruited rock in the service of salvation, although that does not mean that Dylan was wrong to call *Harding* "the first biblical rock album." The problem is that most people focus so much on *Slow Train Coming* that they miss the way Dylan was playing Christian rock a full year before that phrase had even entered the American vocabulary.

Larry Norman should also be given his due. Norman was a maverick who grew up Christian but played in secular bands before deciding to try something new. He wanted to reach out to young people alienated from the slowness of Sunday sounds. Often called "the father of Christian rock," his albums were banned in many Christian bookstores, a fate that would also befall Dylan's *Slow Train Coming*. There are other parallels between Norman and Dylan. Several years after his break-through album, *Only Visiting This Planet* (MGM/Verve, 1972), Norman began turning his back on the music industry. His later albums were not well received, yet his concert performances were subject to numerous bootlegs. Both Dylan and Norman were influenced by Hal Lindsey's study of apocalyptic doom, *The Late Great Planet Earth* (1970). In fact, Norman's most famous song, "I Wish We'd All Been Ready," was the anthem for the Jesus movement throughout the seventies. Norman is some-times linked to Dylan's conversion, because he was associated with the California-based Vineyard Ministries, the organization credited with shaping Dylan's faith. In reality, Norman had noth-ing to do with Dylan's conversion, though Dylan has expressed an admiration for Norman's music.

Besides being old rock warhorses who helped found a new genre of music—Christian rock—that has subsequently all but ignored them, there is a crucial difference between these two. Unlike Dylan, Norman rarely drew upon traditional gospel music for inspiration. Norman never rejected the lyrics of old-fashioned hymns—just their style. By contrast, Dylan's Christian albums are infused with the old gospel sound. Perhaps because Dylan was not raised in the church, he could better appreciate (and appropriate) church music. In any case, his Christian albums, especially *Slow Train Coming*, captured the style of evangelical Christian conviction in a way that will probably never be repeated. The reason is simple. To have an artist of Dylan's stature—someone who had mastered and transformed several genres already, from folk to rock and country and western—throw himself wholeheartedly into the gospel tradition at a crucial stage of his musical development was little short of a miracle. Dylan gave himself totally to Christian music with an innocence and enthusiasm that makes sense only to those who have shared his born-again experience. But the picture is more complex than that. Dylan was reaching middle age when he turned to Christianity. He had experienced the personal failure of a divorce and the artistic failure of his movie, *Renaldo & Clara*, which was roundly criticized and immediately pulled from distribution. He was ready for something new, but he was also returning to something old. He discovered the truth of the gospel message in 1978, but he had long lived in the vicinity of its sound. His critics were speechless, but Dylan had found his voice.

Given Dylan's assessment of *John Wesley Harding*, it is hard not to come to the conclusion that he was a Christian for years before he or anyone else knew it. When Eric Clapton was asked if he was surprised by Dylan's conversion, he replied, "No. I always saw Bob as religious."[13] Yet the religious substance of Dylan's art did not fit with the official history of the sixties and its aftermath. Scholars and journalists neglect and misunderstand evangelical Christianity, even though it has become part of the religious mainstream and has made a lasting impression on the political landscape. In the sixties and seventies, evangelicalism was even more of a mystery to most of the cultural elite than it is today. The media naturally interpreted Dylan in political rather than in religious terms. Even when rock commentators realized the futility of this reading, they persisted with it. Political radicals seem to draw a perverse kind of energy from their love-hate relationship with Dylan. They frame Dylan's career according to a very old-fashioned plot of a paradise lost that was never wholly recovered. According to this scheme, Dylan had an original golden period of leftist idealism followed by various glorious failures to recapture his social relevance. All such narratives must have a low point from which the hero tries one last time for redemption. Dylan's conversion to Christianity serves that purpose in this narrative. It was the ultimate betrayal of his progressive political roots.

Mark Marqusee's book, *Chimes of Freedom: The Politics of Dylan's Art*, is an example of this quixotic attempt to save Dylan from himself by making him look more radical than he ever was. I chose this book for comment not because it is especially misguided in its misreading of Dylan but because it is representative of mainstream scholarship. It is a well-researched, well-written, and well-argued examination of the social context of Dylan's early work, brimming with insights. Nevertheless, reading it is like watching someone repeatedly slam his or her head against a wall. Even worse, Marqusee is at least partially aware of what he is doing, which makes the reader want to intervene and get him to stop. He admits that Dylan drew much of his eccentric syntax from the King James Version of the Bible, and that he structured many of his songs around the call-and-response tradition of the black church. Marqusee also points out how Dylan sought to achieve something otherworldly in his vocal expressions. He even hints at the way Dylan gives voice to the old-fashioned, patriotic idea that America has a unique history and a special destiny to play in the world. Nevertheless, Marqusee speaks for many of Dylan's most dedicated fans when he writes that he became aware of Dylan at the same time that he became aware of himself as a political agent. Try as he might, Marqusee can never manage to separate Dylan's music from his own political passion.

So where does Marqusee's book go wrong? Marqusee dismisses the many comments Dylan has made over the years downplaying or outright denying leftist political convictions. Marqusee's goal is to know Dylan better than Dylan knows himself. Dylan could be a devious interviewee and a sly jokester, as when he told Joan Baez that he wrote "Masters of War" for the money,[14] but at some point, you have to take him at his word. Marqusee, however, has made up his own mind about what Dylan really thinks. "The songs led him to the politics and the politics unlocked his songwriting gifts."[15] He says this in spite of the fact that even in his most topical songs, Dylan wrote about real people, not social types. Dylan did occasionally sacrifice his poetry to make a political point, but when this resulted in sloganeering, he regretted it. For example, he never released his first protest song, "The Death of Emmett Till" (1962), which he soon dismissed as "bullshit."[16]

Marqusee uses a political profile to target every Dylan song. Take, for example, the way he categorizes "Let Me Die in My Footsteps" (1962) as protest music. It was recorded for *The Freewheelin' Bob Dylan* (1963) but was replaced by "Masters of War" and not officially released until the 1991 *Bootleg Series, Volumes 1–3*. Marqusee calls it a "marvelously determined, fresh-faced refusal to take part in the fraud of the civil defense and the larger insanity of the nuclear weapons race."[17] Dylan wrote it after seeing a fallout shelter under construction—these were increasingly common after the 1961 Berlin Wall crisis—but interpretation of his lyrics should not rest at this literal level. Dylan is not above using the image of a bomb shelter to dig deeper into human nature than politics would permit.

Like all great poems, "Let Me Die in My Footsteps" plays with ambiguity. Going "down under the ground" can evoke a bomb shelter or a grave, but fixing its meaning by the coordinates of the Cold War, as Marqusee does, is nothing more than leftist fundamentalism. This song uses a cluster of images to portray a ghostly walker whose slow and steadfast movement close to the ground is indicative of an attitude of stubborn pride. As the first stanza shows, the singer has no other goal than to make his death his own:

> I will not go down under the ground
> 'Cause somebody tells me that death's comin' 'round
> An' I will not carry myself down to die
> When I go to my grave my head will be high
> Let me die in my footsteps
> Before I go down under the ground.

The imagery here is simple only on its surface. The singer wants to die standing up, so to speak. That is, he will not lie down and accept death on death's terms. The song does allude to the demand of the civil authorities that the public seek protection during testing of the siren-system warning of a nuclear attack, but this allusion merely reinforces the singer's determination to die on his own terms. Dylan's song is as little about fallout shelters as Robert Frost's "The Road Not Taken" is about hiking.

Marqusee has to reach back into Dylan's childhood to buttress his interpretation of this song. He speculates about the impact that Cold War scares must have had on an impressionably young Dylan. "As a teenager in Hibbing [Minnesota]," Marqusee imagines, "Bob Dylan had been struck by the surreally inhuman logic of the fallout shelter boom—and he was not alone."[18] In *Chronicles*, Dylan discusses "Let Me Die in My Footsteps" in terms that read like a direct response to Marqusee, whose book was published the year before Dylan's autobiography. Dylan calls the song "slightly ironic" and refutes the idea that it had a radical political message. In northern Minnesota, he explains, nobody built fallout shelters. "As far as communists went," he states dryly, "there wasn't any paranoia about them."[19] Homes had thick basement walls. All you needed for a nuclear attack, he reminisced, was a surplus Geiger counter.

Dylan claims he even had one in his New York apartment. Some might take this for more evidence of Dylan's propensity toward verbal jousting and periodic reinvention, but evidence for how playfully he approached the public safety craze can be found on the cover of *Bringing It All Back Home* (1965). Dylan is surrounded by a beautiful woman (his manager's wife) and an odd assortment of tokens from his life, including a fallout shelter sign.

Nonetheless, "Let Me Die in My Footsteps" is not without political relevance. The middle stanzas express cynicism toward the establishment ("someone is pullin' the wool over me"), and the third to the last stanza talks about throwing "all the guns and the tanks in the sea / For they are mistakes of a past history." It is important to notice, however, that war is an issue in this song only because its threat lets us off the hook of our own imminent death. The second stanza, for example, talks about "rumors of war and wars that have been," as well as how "some people thinkin' that the end is close by." The point is that those who preach a religious or a nuclear apocalypse are mistaken. "'Stead of learnin' to live they are learnin' to die." To truly live, Dylan is saying, we must be willing to face death with every step we take. This is an existential rebuttal to all those who make the worry over war more fundamental than the decision each individual must make about how he or she wants to die.

In the last stanza, Dylan celebrates America in terms that would be rather surprising if this song were an anti-war rant:

Go out in your country where the land meets the sun
See the craters and the canyons where the waterfalls run
Nevada, New Mexico, Arizona, Idaho
Let every state in this union seep down in your souls
And you'll die in your footsteps
Before you go down under the ground.

Clearly, the singer wants to die as he treads softly on the earth—on his own terms and in his own space. That space is none other than the United States of America. It is noteworthy that Dylan does not treat the American landscape as if it were one rolling and continuous whole. He names specific western states and advises us to let their geography become a part of our identity. His use of the phrase "every state in the union" calls attention to America's most tragic event, which did more than anything else to make land sacred in America. Indeed, this song resonates with the sacrifices of the Civil War—not the constraints of the Cold War—which is unsurprising given Dylan's habit during this period of reading newspapers from that era. The Union was preserved by the blood of soldiers who consecrated its ground. If we treat the land of every state of the Union as sacred, we can rest content with death. To die in your footsteps is to die knowing where you stand. True patriotism coincides with a noble and honest death.

Far from being anti-war in any straightforward manner, this song honors the war dead for making the soil sacred. America is the land where our ancestors died and the ground into which we will someday be laid. This song is an example of how Dylan could be critical of war and yet avoid falling into the trap of the kind of anti-Americanism that marginalized so much of radical politics beginning in the late sixties. Dylan loved the way America sounded too much to be anti-American. For Dylan, American music was something new that broke into the auditory history of the world. America sounds different from other countries because America *is* different. Like Woody Guthrie, even when Dylan is criticizing America, you can hear the devotion in his voice overriding the anger.

Marqusee is right that "Let Me Die in My Footsteps" is one of the greatest of the many unnoticed masterpieces from Dylan's early period. He is wrong, however, about its subject matter. "Let Me Die in My Footsteps" can be considered one of the greatest twentieth-century American songs to deal directly with death. This song has even more to say to us today, because people rarely visit cemeteries and do not often consider the idea that land is precious because it holds us when we die.

"With God on Our Side" fits Marqusee's thesis better, because it directly addresses American imperialism. This song begins with a nod to Dylan's roots ("The country I come from / is called the Midwest") and goes stanza by stanza in a workmanlike manner through the history of America's wars. Nonetheless, this apparently straightforward song ends on an ambivalent note. The second to the last stanza is theological, not political:

> Through many dark hour
> I've been thinkin' about this
> That Jesus Christ
> Was betrayed by a kiss
> But I can't think for you
> You'll have to decide
> Whether Judas Iscariot
> Had God on his side.

That stanza shatters the genre of the song, so much so that in the next and last stanza, Dylan admits that he is confused and "weary as Hell." Nobody, he says, can guess the words that fill his head. No wonder, given this provocation about Judas. The stanza about Judas comes completely out of left field—unless all along the song has been more about God than warfare. If this were a protest song, why would it end with the singer confessing confusion? And what are we to make of the intrusion of Judas?

The clue to these questions is found in the very first stanza, where Dylan declares his geographical roots. Dylan is exploring Calvin's doctrine of Providence in this song, not the political left's commitment to pacifism. If you are born in the Midwest, he is saying, this is how you see the world. Far from being a call to change the world, the song insinuates the possibility that change is illusory. Of course midwesterners believe that God is on their side! How could they not? The way geography is origin as well as destination is a trope for the irrefutability of the doctrine of Providence.

But if geography is destiny, then wars fought over geographical borders might be as futile as they are inevitable. That is where Judas comes in. Far from being an example of the use and abuse of free will, Judas confirms the impossibility of thwarting God's will. If God did not intend for Judas to betray Jesus, then there cannot be any substance to the doctrine of divine Providence. Without that doctrine, history has no plot and it is impossible to tell where God stands. But if God did lead Judas to his fateful kiss, then Judas was right, in a way, to think that he was doing the right thing. And if God is on the side of Judas, then whose side is God *not* on? We ordinarily think that God is only on the side of the good guys, but Dylan's train of thought tears asunder such preconceptions. There is protest in this song, but Dylan has totally shifted the foundation for political critique. We do not know whose side God is ultimately on because God's plan transcends human understanding. If God could be on the side of Judas, then God can stand with anybody. Most Dylan fans think of this song as a criticism of any kind of faith in God, since that faith can lead to self-righteous patriotism (i.e., the claim that if God is for us, then God must be against our enemies). On the contrary, it is faith in God that forces us to be more modest about what we can know about history.

Another classic sixties protest song often mistakenly interpreted as a tract on pacifism is "Masters of War." In an interview with Robert Hilburn, Dylan claimed, "There's no anti-war sentiment in that song. I'm not a pacifist. I don't think I've ever been one."[20] When Dylan talks like this, some critics simply do not take him at his word. Others think he is merely pointing out the way "Masters of War" rages against the military-industrial complex (a phrase originated by President Dwight Eisenhower in his last year of office), not the military itself. That distinction is not insignificant. People from all points on the political spectrum could worry about the growing percentage of the nation's capital devoted to the arms buildup. Even this distinction, however, fails to get to the heart of Dylan's protest. Dylan is castigating the armament makers not as much for what they do as for how they do it. Deception is the root of evil, Dylan seems to be saying: "Like Judas of old / You lie and deceive." There is a long history in Christianity of associating Judas with Satan, since they share the stigma of betrayal. That the song is about Satan and not Boeing is signaled by the line, "Even Jesus would never / Forgive what you do." Only Satan, according to some but not all theological traditions, is beyond forgiveness. The military industry is a trope for the ultimate clash of good and evil, which is why Dylan can end the song with the most concise piece of vitriol he ever wrote: "And I hope that you die / And your death'll come soon." He is not expressing his desire to literally kill all of the people who work in the military industry. He is directing his rage against something—or someone—much more fundamental than that. Ironically, Dylan has been criticized for being overly judgmental in his explicitly Christian albums, but this song is the most bitterly accusative he has ever written

More examples of Marqusee's misreadings of Dylan could be examined. He makes way too much of "Talkin' John Birch Paranoid Blues," for example. Written in 1962, it is a piece of social satire that picks on an easy target that even conservatives found embarrassing. There is no evidence that Dylan ever worried about McCarthyism, however, and the fact that he cancelled an appearance on *The Ed Sullivan Show* when the network refused to let him play it on national TV is testimony to his artistic integrity, not his leftist credentials. How Dylan came to write this song, which was the first he published, is revealing. In 1962, Pete Seeger introduced him to the editors of a new magazine, *Broadside*. Their mission was to publish topical songs with a politically radical message. Dylan was hungry for recognition and the opportunity to develop his art. His only patrons at the time were the old lefties who ran the magazine. It is not cynical or dismissive of his early work to say that he knew what he had to do to get ahead.

If Dylan had been a committed political radical, he would have sung out against the Vietnam War. It is revealing, then, that the only reference to Vietnam in his early years is in the beat-inspired liner notes he wrote for *Bringing It All Back Home*, where he tells the story of a pharmacist who accuses him of "causing all the riots over vietnam [*sic*]." In a 1968 interview with the left-wing folk magazine *Sing Out!*, Dylan finally broke his silence about the Vietnam War, and he nearly broke his reputation as well. In fact, the interview reads like a boxing match. The interviewers push him to take a stand. They recite a flurry of grievous sins being committed in America's name, but Dylan ducks their swings and remains impassive and unimpressed. Dylan finally bursts out, "I know some very good artists who are for the war." He is now getting upset, although surely he knew what he was in for when he signed on with the interview. He denies that being "for or against the war" really matters. "That really doesn't exist," he says. They finally push him to the ropes by asking why he does not argue with his painter friend who supports the war. This question leaves them open and vulnerable, because they are assuming that Dylan is against the war. He deflects their question in a defensive and evasive manner. "I can see what goes into his paintings, and why should I?" He is completely uncooperative, and at that point, he unloads his own heavy blow to their heady idealism: "Anyway, how do you know I'm not, as you say, *for* the war?"[21] Marqusee calls this interview sheer perversity, and accuses Dylan of being "lazily satisfied with facile evasions."[22] To me, Dylan does not seem lazy in this interview. He is cornered and he strikes back. Indeed, he asks a pointed question, and it is Marqusee who is being evasive. How does Marqusee know that Dylan was not for the war?

Dylan was not always that angry with the political left. More often, he could be something of a political agnostic, which explains why he felt put-upon while he was living in seclusion in Woodstock after his 1966 motorcycle accident. Young people across America were waiting to hear a defining word from their poet, but he was either keeping his own counsel or not saying what his fans wanted to hear. He even went out of his way to avoid having anything to do with the rock festival that was held nearby (in part to draw him out of his apparent retirement from the rock scene). This withdrawal from public attention only fed the media frenzy. When the public turns somebody into a myth, it can just as easily demonize as divinize him or her. The same people who professed their undying loyalty to him could quickly turn to scorning him. "It seems like the world has always needed a scapegoat," Dylan wryly observes in *Chronicles*. "Whatever the counterculture was, I'd seen enough of it. I was sick of the way my lyrics had been extrapolated, their meanings subverted into polemics and that I had been anointed as the Big Bubba of Rebellion, High Priest of Protest, the Czar of Dissent, the Duke of Disobedience, Leader of the Freeloaders, Kaiser of Apostasy, Archbishop of Anarchy, the Big Cheese."[23] Dylan instinctively resisted being what others wanted to make of him, but he was particularly fierce in fighting the sixties counterculture, which wanted to mock him as their king.

One of his trickiest and oddest public performances could be interpreted as his farewell address to the political left—if there were any evidence that he was a man of the left in the first place. On December 13, 1963, Dylan attended a fundraising dinner for the National Emergency Civil Liberties Committee (NECLC), where he received the group's Tom Paine Award. The NECLC had been established in 1951 to promote free speech and support those who become victims of its suppression, and it was dominated by old leftists who had fought in the trenches against McCarthyism. Dylan, to say the least, made a spectacle of himself. He had one too many drinks at the bar, perhaps to help him overcome his nervousness about public speaking, but as a result, his tongue was loosened and the words did fly. He later told Nat Hentoff that the people in the audience that night wore "minks and jewels, and it was like they were giving money out of guilt."[24] Transcripts of the speech, which can be found on various Web sites, show Dylan in a fighting mood. He begins by announcing that it is not an old peoples' world. That remark gets some laughter. But he goes on to question his audience's sincerity about supporting blacks. He says he does not see any colors at all when he looks at people. "There's no black and white, left and right to me anymore; there's only up and down and down is very close to the ground. And I'm trying to go up without thinking about anything trivial such as politics." He insinuates that blacks have to wear suits in order to get respect from this crowd. "My friends don't have to wear suits." He even recounts his participation in the civil rights march on Washington where he sang on the platform and "looked around at all the Negroes there and I didn't see any Negroes that looked like none of my friends." He obviously felt that the old left wanted blacks to fit into their agenda rather than just accepting them as they are. He went on to express sympathy for Lee Harvey Oswald, which got boos and hisses. This was a classic case of Dylan's testing the limits of his audience. The political left spoke about acceptance and tolerance, but Dylan knew they had no real interest in trying to get inside the head of someone like Oswald.

Needless to say, the speech was a bomb, and the dinner did not raise the expected funds. As a kind of apology, Dylan wrote "A Message" to the group, where he confessed his fears about public speaking. He wanted to run out the door after he finished eating and jump in front of a car rather than give a speech. But Dylan did not retract his words. Instead, he harps on the theme of personal responsibility. He writes that he is "sick so sick at hearin 'we all share the blame'" for all of society's ills and that it is too easy to say "we" and "bow our heads together," as if there is no evil in the world. If there is violence, he argues, there is violence within each of us. He reiterates his point about blacks having to look respectable in order to get respect. And he tells the good folks of the NECLC that he is tired of newspapers and politics. It was a harsh way to say good-bye to the leftist crowd.

He kept saying good-bye to those on the political left, but they behaved like a besotted suitor who couldn't take no for an answer. As early as 1964, in "My Back Pages," he confessed that he "was so much older then / I'm younger than that now," because he realized he had been trying to be something he was not. He goes on to admit that he used to have "A self-ordained professor's tongue," but now he knows he is not qualified to tell others what to think. He also realizes that he did not understand how he could be his own enemy "In the instant that I preach." In other words, he should have been trying to change himself before he tried to change anyone else.

In a poem called "For Dave Glover" printed in the 1963 Newport Folk Festival program, Dylan talked about how easy it used to be to choose sides in political debates. When Woody Guthrie wrote his songs, it was "The American way or the Fascist way. . . . It was that easy." Now, he laments, there are too many sides to choose from. "I don know what happened cause I wasn't around but somewhere along the line . . . things got messed up / More kinds a sides come int' the story / Folks I guess started switchin sides an makin up their own sides." Somehow, he writes, "all sides lost their purpose an folks forgot about other folks." While many of his peers thought the political options were awfully clear and simple, Dylan thought they were putting categories and labels ahead of feelings and people.

His rejection of leftist politics was reinforced by a visit to Princeton University in 1970 to accept an honorary doctorate of music. This act of toadying to the Ivy League outraged the underground press. If he had gone to Hanoi to shake hands with the communists, they would have embraced him as a prodigal son returning home. The underground press was probably right to interpret the Princeton visit as an affront. The left put so much pressure on him that he had to cope by keeping his fans guessing about what he was doing and who he was. He stopped taking their ideas and questions seriously and, in what was perhaps the most radical gesture he could have made, he refused to think that his political opinions were all that important. This drove some fans crazy, which seems to have happened literally to A. J. Weberman, a college dropout who invented the science of "garbology" in a perverse attempt to discover why Dylan was so far removed from the political action. He was disappointed by what he found in Dylan's New York City garbage pail in 1970. "Nowhere did I find any evidence that Dylan was at all interested in politics, causes, activism or world affairs."[25] Weberman might have been crazy in the way he stalked Dylan, but at least he was candid about Dylan's politics. He grew so frustrated with Dylan's lack of interest in social or cultural revolution that he formed the Dylan Liberation Front in an attempt to save Dylan from himself.

His leftist fans were turning Dylan into a scapegoat, as he observes in *Chronicles*. They were looking for a political hero in what were decidedly unheroic times. Recognizing the political pressure Dylan was under leads to a rereading of one of his most raucous songs. American and British radio stations banned "Rainy Day Women #12 & 35" because they thought it was a drug song, and it certainly sounds that way. Released on *Blonde on Blonde* (1966), the loopy music has the zany atmosphere of a circus, but the lyrics point in another direction.

> Well, they'll stone ya when you're trying to be so good
> They'll stone ya just a-like they said they would
> They'll stone ya when you're tryin' to go home

Then they'll stone ya when you're there all alone
But I would not feel so all alone
Everybody must get stoned

Read closely, the lyrics speak more of persecution than intoxica-tion. Even the cacophonous music, from this perspective, sounds like a Salvation Army band playing a funeral march, albeit after one drink too many. Stoning, of course, was an ancient custom of execution recorded in the Bible. Near the end of the song, Dylan says they will stone you "when you are set down in your grave." This is hardly a drug song. At most, it is a parody of a drug song, with Dylan and the musicians having a laugh at trying to sound like what people who have never been high might think it sounds like to be on drugs. Within that par-ody, however, is one of the most tragic (and Christian) messages that Dylan has ever sung: when you try to be good in this world, you get killed. This message is so serious that Dylan could have sung it only under the cover of what sounds like a carnival. The carnival sound is appropriate, moreover, because it is in such drunken revelries that somebody is most vulnerable to being stalked, scapegoated, and stoned to death.

In response to stalkers like Weberman, Dylan's various ob-fuscations about his life and his music were a necessary strategy of self-protection (and a way of protecting his family), but his constant motion through the musical world could also add to his allure. Some people have accused him of changing with the times in order to capitalize on new musical trends, while others see him as a musical magician who could change the direction rock was heading through the sheer force of his will. Even his Christian conversion can be subjected to this debate. After all, he found his way to an evangelical faith at just the time that evangelicals were finding their way into the popular culture. This is shortsighted. Dylan was always changing, but throughout his career, he gave consistent musical expression to a set of core theological and political convictions. The core of his core convictions, as his so-called anti-war songs indicate, is a sense of the tragic inevitability of human failure coupled with an emphasis on personal responsibility.

That core of the core is none other than a musical translation of the Christian doctrine of original sin, which describes human freedom as being bound by fault and fallibility. Sin is original not simply because of its origin in Adam and Eve but because it originates in our every effort to deny that we are sinful. That is a subtle and scary insight, but it has inspired much of the greatest art and literature in Western history. Dylan stands in that tradition, not least because of his attitude toward politics. The arena of politics is necessary only as a response to a world gone wrong. It is human nature to react to sin with the incessant compromises and blame shifting of politics, but it is part of our redeemed nature to take personal responsibility for our actions. The paradoxical idea that we are free and yet bound to sin has its counterpart in the idea that we alone are responsible for our sin, even though we can only be saved by God's aid. The politics of original sin can lead to a gloomy sense of futility, but for the most part, Christian tradition has kept the emphasis on personal responsibility. This emphasis is the key to Dylan's refusal to be identified with the political left.

Like everyone else in the sixties, Dylan was wondering, as he put it in the "Ballad of Donald White," whether criminals were "enemies or victims of your society?" The political left answered that question by blaming society for social deviancy. Rather than looking for historical and structural causes for societal ills, Dylan, like conservative Christians at that time, unfashionably preached personal responsibility. "Who Killed Davey Moore?" goes right to the heart of the question of personal responsibility by analyzing the basic human tendency to play hot potato by passing the blame around. This song is about the death of a boxer in the ring, and nobody, from the referee and the crowd to his manager, the gamblers, the sportswriters, and the other boxer who launched the fatal blow, will take responsibility for his death. If nobody killed him, Dylan is asking, then how could he be dead? Individuals, rather than collective social forces, must be to blame.

Some of his best songs from the sixties were radical transformations of the blame game. "Only a Pawn in Their Game" is almost devious in the way that it upsets the listener's expectations. Dylan performed this song for an African-American audience at a voter registration drive on Silas Magee's farm in Greenwood, Mississippi, on July 6, 1963. The performance was filmed, and a segment of it was included in D. A. Pennebaker's documentary *Don't Look Back* (1967), which helped established Dylan's credentials as a civil rights activist. Dylan could not have chosen a more inappropriate song for this cotton patch concert—if, that is, he was really trying to advertise his allegiance to the left. He wrote it after Medgar Evers was murdered in the spring of 1963, at a time when northern liberals were pointing their fingers in unison at all southern whites. "Only a Pawn in Their Game" turns these fingers back at the pointers. In a song that is supposed to be about a black civil rights martyr, Dylan actually defends southern whites.

> And the poor white remains
> On the caboose of the train
> But it ain't him to blame
> He's only a pawn in their game.

This is an audacious argument to make in the political climate of 1963. Southern whites are not the object of Dylan's disdain, just as blacks are not the object of his pity. This song is about how the political and cultural elite on both sides of the Mason-Dixon line victimize poor, rural whites. Poor whites are targets of political manipulation just as blacks are victims of racism. Dylan even extends sympathy for Evers's killer. Dylan observes that while "they lowered him [Evers] down as a king," the killer, a white man, goes nameless. This is a protest song, but it does not fit the protest genre. Dylan is protesting against the way Evers's murder was being used to stereotype an entire class of people. Rather than pointing his finger at the South, he was holding up a mirror to the North.

Two other songs are examples of the complexity of Dylan's moral imagination. "I Shall Be Free No. 10" is one of the most daunting songs Dylan ever wrote. It begins with a nod to equality: "I'm just average, common too / I'm just like him, the same as you." Then the singer/narrator of the song gets comical by saying that he is going to outbox Cassius Clay. This clearly makes the singer seem delusional. The third stanza is the key to the song:

> Now, I'm liberal, but to a degree
> I want ev'rybody to be free
> But if you think that I'll let Barry Goldwater
> Move in next door and marry my daughter
> You must think I'm crazy!
> I wouldn't let him do it for all the farms in Cuba.

A casual listener might think that Goldwater is being ridiculed, but the opposite is the case. Remember, the singer thinks he can beat the heavyweight champion of the world, so he is a bit crazy. He is crazy because he thinks that, though he is average and common, he can do anything he wants. He thinks everyone is equal, but he also thinks he is more equal than anyone. He is, in other words, an egomaniac. Keeping in mind that Dylan actually liked Barry Goldwater in the sixties, the song makes sense. Liberals think of themselves as free from prejudice, but they have just as many hang-ups as the conservatives. A liberal would not let Goldwater marry his daughter even if it meant the liberation of Cuba. That, Dylan is insinuating, is not only an indication of prejudice. It is also really crazy. After several more nonsensical stanzas, Dylan pens a blistering critique of country club liberals:

I'm gonna grow my hair to my feet so strange
So I look like a walking mountain range
And I'm gonna ride into Omaha on a horse
Out to the country club and the golf course
Carry the *New York Times*, shoot a few holes, blow their minds

This was written years before conservatives began picking apart liberal hypocrisy. That Dylan did not expect his (largely liberal) fans to understand his lyrics is clear in the next and last stanza, where he sings, "Now you're probably wondering by now / Just what this song is all about." This song contradicts his audience's expectations in such a perverse way that Dylan had little hope of being understood.

The other song that exemplifies moral complexity to a degree that breaks through the typical rock format is "Talkin' World War III Blues." This song makes fun of paranoia on the left in a way that complements his parody of the John Birch Society, although this is rarely pointed out. Dylan is merciless in his criticism of the way some people can be so obsessed with the fear of nuclear war that they no longer know how to function in ordinary society. The song begins as a crazy dream but ends with everybody having the same dream, which demonstrates how irrational fear can spread like a contagion. The parody here is gentle—Dylan likes crazy people—but it demonstrates that Dylan was keeping his distance from both extremes of the political spectrum. For Dylan, the question was always—as another of his early songs put it—"Whatcha Gonna Do," not who are you going to blame or what movement are you going to join.

Although his political songs after his conversion to Christianity have not received much positive attention, they continue his exploration of the way many people use the language of politics to avoid personal responsibility. To translate this insight into Christian terms, people inevitably use their reason to rationalize their sinfulness. "Political World" from *Oh Mercy* (1989) is often taken as a departure from his youthful idealism (Dylan never had any youthful idealism to depart from), but it should be heard instead as a masterful summation of his political philosophy. The message of the song is that politics is the problem, not the answer. The key to this claim comes in the first stanza:

> We live in a political world
> Love don't have any place
> We're living in times where men commit crimes
> And crime don't have a face.

Crime is faceless because we assign responsibility to impersonal social forces rather than to individuals. In a political world, "wisdom is thrown into jail." When people refuse to take responsibility for their own actions, "you're trained to take what looks like the easy way out." The song ends by inviting us to shout God's name, but in a political world, "you're never sure what it is." If we do not begin with knowledge of our own sin, we cannot properly know who God is.

Self-knowledge is hard. It is certainly harder than blaming others for your fate. Nonetheless, this emphasis on personal responsibility does not preclude a critique of social institutions. Instead, focusing on personal sin provides a provocative perspective on the way in which sin accumulates power and influence in social institutions. "Union Sundown" from *Infidels* (1983) is a nuanced reflection on the relationship between individual and social responsibility. On the surface, this song laments the decline of the labor unions. Buying products made in the United States "was a good idea / 'Til greed got in the way." From a lesser songwriter, the song at this point would have turned into a rant against globalization. Dylan veers away from that line of analysis just when the listener suspects that's where he's steering. He ends a long stanza on how jobs are shipped overseas with the description of a woman making only thirty cents a day for a family of twelve, and wryly observes, "You know, that's a lot of money to her." The lesson seems to be that multinational corporations are pulling up roots here, but they are employing the poor over there. Unions in America try to keep the jobs here, but Dylan is suspicious. Far from the leftist idealization of unions, Dylan sings, "The unions are big business, friend." Finally, Dylan moves his level of analysis to the heart of the problem, which is not capitalism or politics. "This world is ruled by violence / But I guess that's better left unsaid." Of course, he has said it, but he has also said it in a way that acknowledges that nobody wants to listen to what he has said. What he has said is that there is something fundamentally wrong with human nature that cannot be fixed by politics. What he has said is that people today do not want to dwell on the undeniable reality of original sin—or on the idea that there is a ruler behind the rule of violence.

A commonplace of the historical study of Christianity is that liberal theology emerged in the nineteenth century when church leaders began cutting away at the overgrown doctrine of original sin. Political liberalism followed the path that liberal theology cleared. When human beings are considered essentially good, their perfectibility can be planned by the cultural elite, while their failures are blamed on social obstacles that have not yet yielded to the omnipotent forces of progress. Theological liberalism is thus the necessary prerequisite to political liberalism, although political liberalism since the sixties has jettisoned its theological roots. Dylan was never much drawn to either political or theological liberalism. If anything, the more distance we have from the sixties, the more we can see how persuasive it is to put Dylan on the side of the forces of conservation rather than with the powers of progress and liberation.

The idea of a "Right Wing Bob," as one recent Web site puts it, will be difficult for many of his fans to take. Nonetheless, it makes sense to read an artist against the grain of the usual interpretations when that artist has consistently expressed a contrarian's spirit. Perhaps I am able to put Dylan in a new political perspective because I am a child of the seventies rather than the sixties. Some of my seventies peers feel so overshadowed by the sixties that they are incessantly trying to live up to its imaginary radical ideal, but it is unhealthy to feel nostalgia for somebody else's political convictions. Yet embracing the seventies as an alternative zeitgeist to the sixties would also be a mistake. Indeed, many of the seventies generation are burdened with a mixture of pride and loathing about growing up in the first decade when entertainment became both the medium and the message. Too frequently, the flower children of the sixties left their decade's style but not its spirit, but we survivors of the seventies are reluctant to claim our peculiar unit of time. Perhaps our ambivalence toward the past motivates us to scavenge culture, not politics, for the remains of the traditions that sustained our ancestors.

My point is not to recruit Dylan as a secret coconspirator in the neoconservative plot to take over America. He was not a double agent working in a troubadour's disguise. As I have already argued, it is important to remember that modern-day American conservativism was just being born in the sixties, a development that would not find national political success until the election of Reagan to the presidency in 1980. Few of the intellectual or cultural elite could even imagine a conservative (as opposed to a radical) alternative to the liberal political consensus that had reigned in both parties since World War II. Dylan was critical of the liberal status quo in the sixties, but he had little institutional political edifice to give support to his critique. It is anachronistic to define Dylan's conservatism by the standards of party politics, but it would also be a mistake to think that he rebelled against liberalism only because it happened to be in the ascendancy at the time. Dylan embodied the conservative spirit of honoring the past over the present while being suspicious of secular designs for a perfect future. Dylan was a conservative because he was a radical in his critique of the modern world. Something drew him to make his art a sign of contradiction rather than a sign of the times. Like many great artists, he had a sense of being compelled by a destiny over which he exercised little control. The best way to understand what he was, it follows, is to examine what he became. At the most decisive turning point in his career, he found not a political but a religious framework for his beliefs—and, of course, the priority of religion over politics is one of the central tenets of conservatism. When he finally arrived at an explicit affirmation of Christian faith, it became apparent that the slow train of his conversion had been a long time coming.

Notes

1. G. K. Chesterton, *Saint Thomas Aquinas* (New York: Doubleday, 1956), p. 24.

2. All quotations from Dylan's lyrics are from Bob Dylan, *Lyrics, 1962–2001* (New York: Simon & Schuster, 2004).

3. It has become a commonplace of leftist cultural criticism to bemoan the political passivity induced by rock and roll. Nevertheless, notice the convoluted way that postmodernist social theorist Lawrence Grossberg tries to salvage his love for grinding guitar work: "Rock offers neither salvation nor transcendence, neither an anarchy of fun nor a narcotic of bliss. Rock is a site of temporary investment, without the power to restructure everyday life. But it still produces lines of flight, not only in the face of nihilism but precisely through the forms of nihilism itself." *We Gotta Get Out of This Place: Popular Conservativism and Postmodern Culture* (New York: Routledge, 1992), p. 237. Grossberg is resigned to the fact that rock's only power is the power of escape.

4. Larry David Smith, *Writing Dylan: The Songs of a Lonesome Traveler* (Westport, CT: Praeger Publishers, 2005). Also note how Bryan Cheyette mars his otherwise insightful examination of train imagery in Dylan's work by placing Dylan's Christianity in the context of what Cheyette calls "his serial conversions" in "On the 'D' Train: Bob Dylan's Conversions," *Do You Mr. Jones? Bob Dylan with the Poets and Professors*, ed. Neil Corcoran (London: Chatto & Windus, 2002), pp. 221–52.

5. Stephen Scobie, *Alias Bob Dylan Revisited* (Toronto: Red Deer Press, 2003), p. 136. Dylan pays tribute not to Bruce's immoral lifestyle but to his status as an underappreciated outlaw who told the truth and knew what he was talking about. The message is that Bruce was too radical for those who think they are radical—he was "more of an outlaw than you ever were." Notice the pronoun in the final line: "He was the brother you never had." It is hard not to hear this song as a meditation on Dylan's own troubled relationship with his typical fan base.

6. *Chronicles, Volume One*, p. 283.

7. Edna Gundersen, "The 'Oh Mercy' Interview: Part I," *On the Tracks* 3 (Spring 1994), pp. 12, 14–15 (originally published in *USA Today*, Sept. 21, 1989).

8. Howard Sounes, *Down the Highway: The Life of Bob Dylan* (New York: Grove Press, 2001), pp. 227–28.

9. Stephen Davis, *Old Gods Almost Dead: The 40-Year Odyssey of the Rolling Stones* (New York: Broadway Books, 2001), p. 237.

10. Anthony Scaduto, *Bob Dylan* (1971; London: Helter Skelter Publishing, 2001), p. 249. Scaduto gives one of the best analyses of any single Dylan album in his discussion of *John Wesley Harding* (see pp. 249–57).

11. Neil Hickey, "The TV Guide Interview," *Younger Than That Now: The Collected Interviews with Bob Dylan* (New York: Thunder's Mouth Press, 2004), p. 104.

12. Although, given his fascination with the quality and variety of sound, this might have been an honest answer. He spends several pages in *Chronicles* fondly recounting a time when he met a man who made sound effects for radio shows. *Chronicles*, pp. 49–51.

13. Bauldie, *Wanted Man*, p. 157 (from a 1987 interview by Roger Gibbons originally published in the Surrey *Telegraph*).

14. Joan Baez, *And a Voice to Sing With: A Memoir* (New York: Simon & Schuster, 1987), p. 95.

15. Mike Marqusee, *Chimes of Freedom: The Politics of Dylan's Art* (New York: New Press, 2003), p. 50. This book was reissued in an expanded edition as *Wicked Messenger: Bob Dylan and the 1960s* (New York: Seven Stories Press, 2005). Marqusee continues to interpret Dylan's protest period, short as it was, as the foundation for his entire career. In the revised edition, he adds a section on Dylan's *Chronicles*. He argues that this book demonstrates "an umbilical link" between Dylan and the sixties, yet he also argues that Dylan "seems to be revising his past to reconcile it to his current world view" and that "Dylan's

characterization of the politics of his early days is disingenuous" (pp. 321 and 325). Marqusee cannot accept Dylan's word.

16. Clinton Heylin, *Behind the Shades Revisited* (New York: Harper Collins, 2001), p. 93.

17. Marqusee, *Chimes of Freedom*, p. 52.

18. Ibid., p. 51. Dylan told the story about seeing the fallout shelter under construction to Nat Hentoff in a 1963 interview published as the sleeve notes to *Freewheelin'* and republished in the Dylan fanzine *Telegraph*, vol. 8.

19. *Chronicles*, p. 271.

20. Robert Hilburn, "How Does It Feel? Don't Ask," *Los Angeles Times*, Sept. 16, 2001. Other interesting quotes from this interview: "I'm not sure people understood a lot of what I was writing about." And: ". . . there are people who manipulated the Vietnam War. They were traitors to America, whoever they were."

21. *Sing Out!* interview by John Cohen and Happy Traum in Craig McGregor, ed., *Bob Dylan: The Early Years, a Retrospective* (New York: Da Capo Press, 1990), pp. 265–94.

22. Marqusee, *Chimes of Freedom*, p. 247.

23. *Chronicles*, pp. 115 and 120.

24. Interview with Nat Hentoff, *The New Yorker*, Oct. 24, 1964, reprinted in *Younger Than That Now*, p. 29.

25. A. J. Weberman, *My Life in Garbology* (New York: Stonehill Publishing Company, 1980), p. 8.

CHAPTER THREE

Slow Train
Long Time Coming

When Bob Dylan went electric in the sixties, the folkies would not forgive him. When he became a Christian, the rockers began forgetting him. His most die-hard fans were deaf to the changing of his tune. Much of their criticism of his so-called Christian albums is marred by resentment, ignorance, and misunderstanding. I say "so-called," because it is arguable whether his three central Christian albums—*Slow Train Coming* (1979), *Saved* (1980), and *Shot of Love* (1981)—really stand apart from the rest of his work. More continuities than discontinuities mark his oeuvre. As much as he kept reinventing himself, he also remained very much the same artist. His explicitly Christian songs are more than a canon within a canon—that is, a minor set of unique accomplishments within a larger body of work. Instead, they are the key that unlocks both the musical and the thematic unity of his work as a whole.

The key unlocks the door, but there is a big room on the other side. That is, Dylan's music overflows with themes and ideas, and no label can sum it up. Many critics point to his ambivalence about women as a central musical concern. Dylan often idealizes women while at the same time fearing their ability to sap his artistic strength. Other critics point to his preoccupation with death. His Christian period brings both of these themes to a culmination without forcing them into a neatly packaged resolution. Sexual passion is sublimated into love of God, but there are still plenty of women who are leading him along. Fear of death, meanwhile, is modulated by the hope for heaven, but there is still plenty of righteous anger about the messy state of the world.

The Christian albums do not nullify his earlier songs by providing all the answers to the questions they raise. Nor do they mark the end of his journey. There are answers in the early work, even if they are blowing in the wind, and there are plenty of questions in the explicitly Christian music, with Dylan frequently barely hanging onto his faith. The tensions that make him a true artist do not suddenly disappear when he puts salvation to song. He is still conflicted about the role of women in his life and their power to save or enslave him. He is still struggling with the pressures of fame (or, increasingly, the peculiar pressures of diminishing fame). He is still wondering why people do the things they do, and why self-knowledge is so hard to obtain. Christianity makes the tensions in his earlier work clearer, but faith does not resolve those tensions in a sea of simple slogans. Whatever nonbelievers might think, faith is intellectually and existentially challenging. Faith flourishes in the soil of doubt and despair, or else it would not be faith.

People who experience a deep and sudden conversion to a new set of religious beliefs—even if those beliefs are a culmination of an inquiry that began years before—often find that for the first time they are able to understand intellectually the contradiction they have long experienced existentially between who they are and what they want to be. They understand the depth of their sin and the infinite possibilities of the holiness they are called to embody. Evangelical Christians call this being "born again." Most people who go through this difficult transformation are not subjected to national scrutiny. The born again can be annoying to their neighbors and their coworkers, especially when they wallow in their spiritual walk or hype their holiness, but they are usually tolerated by people who already know them and are willing to give them the benefit of the doubt. When Dylan became born again, he annoyed millions of people who did not know him but thought that they had the right to keep him stuck in a certain place in their minds. Probably no religious conversion in the twentieth century was so publicly analyzed and criticized as this one.

Dylan was as prepared as anyone could be for the fallout, but it still must have been overwhelming. His penchant for contradiction had set up a tension between performer and audience that long preceded his born-again period. Throughout the sixties, he was creating music that was more grounded in the Apostle Paul and the Book of Revelation than in Norman O. Brown's celebration of polymorphous sexual perversity, which was so popular at that time. Before he softened his tone with the country-tinged *Nashville Skyline* (1969), he often used songs to pick a moral argument with his audience. His inclination to take inordinate glee in musical aggression reached its climax in the Christian concerts of 1979–81. When he began preaching from the stage, and not just preaching in his music, many of his fans were dumbfounded. More than a few responded with rude catcalls and boos. Although he was accustomed to disparagement and incomprehension, performing in such conditions must have been daunting. He showed enormous courage during these shows.

The worst of it came when he performed two shows in Tempe, Arizona, in November 1979, to a crowd composed mainly of college students. If you want to rock and roll, he told them, "You can go and see Kiss and you can rock and roll all the way down to the pit!" This was no random comment. Rock concerts are often little more than orchestrations of frenzied fanaticism. Rock stars act in an infantile manner and their fans pay big bucks to see them dramatize mock rage, which facilitates the adolescent fondness for self-destruction. Dylan's anger, however, was the real thing. It was as if an adult suddenly intervened in a teenage pot party. For many paying customers, it was a violation of their right to consumer satisfaction. Dylan had often held his audiences in disdain; now he held them in contempt. Of course, he should have saved his anger for fallen humanity, not his audience, but he should be forgiven for this misdirection of his emotions. After all, the anger fit the songs, and he probably used it to motivate some complex vocal performances that demanded all the skill he could muster. One of the reasons *Slow Train Coming* was so musically effective is that it brought the apocalyptic rage that fueled much of his best early work to a fulsome culmination.

Far from betraying his early work, Dylan found his voice on *Slow Train Coming*. Singing with this kind of range and daring takes confidence bordering on religious faith, and now he had that faith in bucketfuls. Dylan had been on a musical mission all his life, and now he found a cause worthy of his vocal genius. In the sixties, his refusal to make political statements or side with political radicals left a hole in his work. His music was so powerful that it seemed like it should be trumpeting a new movement destined to transform the globe. Yet the only movement that came—the political and cultural left determined to stop the Vietnam War and overthrow traditional morality—was not what Dylan wanted. Dylan had been a believer without a church, heralding a kingdom without a castle. Now he had arrived. As one perceptive critic put it, "On *Slow Train* he slid out of the pew and took to the pulpit."[1] That level of insight, however, was rare among journalists and fans. Most rock critics were allergic to Dylan's faith, which demonstrated how they had been more seduced by his image than by the words of his songs.

Dylan first took his faith public at San Francisco's Warfield Theatre in November 1979, and the naysayers were waiting in ambush. The front-page headline of the *San Francisco Examiner* declared, "Born Again Dylan Bombs," while the *San Francisco Chronicle* chimed in with "Bob Dylan's God-Awful Gospel." The articles that followed were the origin of the myth that fans walked out of these concerts by the droves. More accurate descriptions noted that after some rocky starts, most audiences enjoyed the music, even if they naturally wanted to hear the old hits that Dylan refused to play. One fan picketed outside the theater with a sign that read, JESUS LOVES YOUR OLD SONGS, TOO. It was unheard of for a star of this magnitude to play concerts of totally new music. It was as if Dylan were trying to educate his fans to a new form of hearing. Some resisted, but the journalists were the ones who felt betrayed the most. Dylan had obviously struck a chord that grated on their nerves.

To be fair to the San Francisco newspapers, critical responses to Dylan's work (with the exception of *Blood on the Tracks*, 1975) had been going downhill for most of the seventies. Still, the vehemence surrounding his Christian concerts was extravagant, but then again, it was an extravagant decade. The change of style that drew such a strong critical reaction came at a low point in American popular culture. To take but one example, the spate of trucker movies that had been dominating box offices throughout the seventies evolved in 1979 into the trucker-with-chimp concept in the hit TV series *B.J. and the Bear*. Musically, disco had made its way to the Midwest, and the great backlash, involving chants of "disco sucks," had begun. That backlash sounds silly today, but it was serious then, and it portended the new mood of the eighties. Disco stood for urban sexual looseness. It was music made for messing around.

Organized criticisms of it were the first sign that people were in the mood to use popular culture to make traditional moral arguments, not illicit love. Political conservatives had been demolished at the polls in 1964 with Goldwater's defeat and had struggled against Nixon and Ford in their own party, but now they were on the warpath. More specifically, evangelical Christianity had become a political force with Ronald Reagan's candidacy for president. Much of the rest of the nation was just becoming acquainted with Reagan in 1979, but California residents knew him well as their ex-governor. Given this cultural climate, testifying to your faith in public was not just a matter of sharing your personal experience. By this time in the nation's history, witnessing for Jesus was fighting words.

Dylan's critics thought they heard in his gospel music yet another example of the bad taste that was endemic in the seventies. After all, here was a white man sounding like he was at a black revival meeting. Contemporary black musicians were playing funk, not gospel. Gospel was getting no respect in the black entertainment community, so why would a white guy get any kudos for trying to revive it? Even though many could not understand Dylan's choice, his long apprenticeship to the black gospel tradition had earned him the moral prerogative to make it his own. The most distinguishing characteristic of black preaching that Dylan borrowed—and not just in his talking blues songs—is the fusion of speech and song. The black sermon amplifies the inherently melodic and rhythmic aspects of the human voice, bringing public speaking to an emotional climax in the affirming response of the congregation. All of rock and roll is in debt to the call-and-response structure of African-American worship, but Dylan is the one white singer who has perfected the black preacher's ability to straddle the line between singing and talking. One aspect of black preaching that has rarely been mentioned in connection with Dylan's style is the way black preachers elongate their syllables and vowels for emphasis.

Especially in Dylan's early songs, the plain speaking of white folk music and the elasticity of black vocal theatrics come together to create a new form of musical proclamation. Nevertheless, Dylan has been selective in his appropriations of the black preaching style. The way black preachers can make rapid ascents into hollering and other vocal embellishments has influenced much rock, but not Dylan's more controlled style.

The black community itself would not recreate gospel until Kirk Franklin released his debut album in 1993. *Kirk Franklin & the Family* was the first gospel record to sell over a million copies. Franklin fused gospel and hip-hop in a way that demolishes the boundary between the sacred and the secular. Discussions abound about whether Franklin stretches the gospel tradition out of any recognizable shape, but then again, Thomas Dorsey's music was also innovative for its time. What had really changed was the maturation of evangelical Christianity. Christian singers could be bolder about appropriating secular styles because conservative churches were being aggressive in using music to reach a wider audience. While Franklin's music has been controversial in some black churches, Dylan's gospel albums never really penetrated white or black churches with any depth. He was, perhaps, too early with his revolution. Perhaps, too, his gospel sound was too gospel; it certainly was more traditionally rooted than Franklin's more contemporary feel.

On the other hand, perhaps Dylan's gospel albums were not radical enough. That is, his Christian music was in a way a distillation of his previous work, but by making explicit what had hitherto been implicit, he troubled many of his fans. Those who did not want to acknowledge that he had always been more than a little bit gospel were the ones who most rejected his new sound. Lou Adler, a music executive steeped in gospel tradition, was one of those who heard the gospel in Dylan long before Dylan turned gospel. Adler produced an African-American group called "The Brothers and Sisters" singing Dylan songs in the gospel style, but the result, *Dylan's Gospel* (first released in 1969), was too eccentric to garner any attention at the time. True, some of the songs work better than others. It is hard to listen to "Lay, Lady, Lay" sung as a Sunday morning hymn. Nonetheless, the ease with which Adler nudged some of Dylan's classic work down the gospel path is richly suggestive of Dylan's own musical background. Adler gives the lead vocals to his female singers, and the change of gender brings a joyful air to Dylan's songs. Adler also slows the tempo of the songs, so that they do not sound like they are in a hurry to get anywhere. By structuring the songs around a chorus, he brings out the dynamic of call-and-response that is often present in a hidden way in Dylan's early music. Some of the songs suffer from that seventies upbeat treatment and thus sound a bit too happy. Others sound too much like the Motown formula, with the background singers assuring you that everything is going to be groovy. Who would have thought that you could clap your hands to a Dylan tune? Dylan never mentions this album in interviews, but it must have had an impact on his decision to use black female backup singers during his Christian recordings and concerts. In fact, during the early eighties he dated one of his backup singers, Clydie King, who was one of the members of "The Brothers and Sisters" chorus that performed on *Dylan's Gospel*.

That this record could be reissued in 2000 is a measure of how our ears have changed. We are more receptive to the gospel sound today, thanks in part to Kirk Franklin's genre-bending revival. Listening to *Dylan's Gospel* today is odd because it both conjures up nostalgia for the early seventies and forces a new perspective on Dylan's work from the sixties. It sounds silly and revolutionary at the same time, if that is possible

A similar recording is *Gotta Serve Somebody: The Gospel Songs of Bob Dylan* (2003), which is performed in the black evangelical style by some of the best Christian musicians in the country. This album, however, is less challenging than *Dylan's*

Gospel, because it does not have as far to go in its musical journey. It takes songs that are already in the black evangelical style and embellishes them with more of the same. Dylan wrote the songs on *Slow Train Coming* with the intention of having Carolyn Dennis, a black gospel singer, record them. (Dylan had a child with Dennis and married her in 1986. They divorced several years later.) *Gotta Serve Somebody* sticks fairly close to the original versions of Dylan's songs, but there are some surprises nonetheless. Given that Dylan's vocal range has become more restricted as he grows older, some of the renditions on this album are reminders of the audacity of much of Dylan's music. Dottie Peoples, for example, shows what a vocal workout "I Believe in You" can be, and she is more than up to the task. And Aaron Neville brings his sweet sound to "Saving Grace." Neville has his own inimitable style, completely unlike Dylan's. While Dylan's vocal variations within a song can be abrupt, Neville dances around the notes like Fred Astaire. If Dylan's voice can sound at times like it is all in the end of his nose, Neville's sounds like it is emanating from the top of his head, pitched high and light. Neville is as soft as Dylan is hard.

Even when Dylan is at his best, there are things his voice cannot do. Only a black gospel singer can hold a perfectly pitched note for a long time and then suddenly turn it into a guttural cry. This mixture of the suffering and the sublime is characteristic of the black gospel sound. Gospel singers can go from joy to sorrow in the plink of a piano key, which helps explain why *Gotta Serve Somebody*, like *Dylan's Gospel*, brings out a wide range of emotions in Dylan's Christian songs. When Dylan performs them, he is trying to prove something. These black singers sound as if they are more comfortable with the words. Black gospel music is legitimized by the power of the black churches. This organic connection to a social institution enables black gospel music to overcome the distinction between high and low culture, as well as sacred and secular. Black gospel music can be entertaining and pedagogical, as well as spiritual and sassy, at the same time. Having said all of this, it is still refreshing to come to the last song on this album, where Dylan himself steps in to perform a duet with Mavis Staples on "Gonna Change My Way of Thinking." Here we have a little rock and roll, driven by guitars and drum, rather than the more gospel sound of the piano that appears on the other songs on the album. We are back in Dylan-land, which is neither church nor tavern but somewhere half way between.

That *Slow Train Coming* is real gospel music is demonstrated by how little effort it took to "blacken" it in *Gotta Serve Somebody*. White musicians have long dipped into African-American resources to rejuvenate popular music, but to the cultural elite, Dylan had dipped too deeply and gotten caught trying to sell the real thing. What they did not understand is that Dylan was part of a wider reaction to a period of moral meaninglessness. Dylan himself had contributed to the narcissism of the seventies with the self-indulgent movie *Renaldo & Clara* as well as with some albums that were mostly disposable. Now, however, he was trying to call a halt to the low-life proceedings that passed for entertainment by moving his fans to a higher musical plane. Black Christianity was born out of a protest against brutality and hypocrisy. Dylan was using it to protest the cultural decadence of the seventies. Far from being an exercise in selling out, Dylan's Christian music was full of cultural critique. Those who censured Dylan were being reactionary by trying to protect the status quo.

The one principal exception to the dominion of spiritually deaf rock critics is Paul Williams. A longtime Dylan fan, Williams reacted to the news of Dylan's conversion with the speed of someone jumping into a river to save a drowning man. Dylan was his hero, and Williams was determined to save his reputation. Williams saw seven of the famous Warfield concerts in eight days, and he knew the critics were missing something. He immediately began writing a book. He finished *Dylan—What Happened?* in two weeks and had it published a month later.[2] Dylan could not have found a better public relations representative if he had hired one himself.

The result is one of the most remarkable acts of listening in the history of rock journalism. Williams was not a Christian, so he was not one of the few who showed up at the San Francisco concerts predisposed to side with Dylan's theology. Nonetheless, he managed to really hear what Dylan had to say. Partly this was a product of Williams's belief that his hero could do no wrong. That belief could have blinded him to some of Dylan's faults, but in this case, it allowed him to transcend the prejudiced reactions that were so common among other diehard fans. The book explains his main reaction to the new music: gratitude that Dylan is letting his audience into his inner life more than at any point in his career.

At times, Williams can almost sound like a theologian in his short book. He observes how Dylan "pushed conscious creation to its limit and found that at the next highest level you have to be a servant again."[3] Williams also helpfully distinguishes between confidence and conviction. He observes that Dylan had tons of confidence in the seventies—perhaps too much, given how he made some slothful artistic decisions—but was running short of conviction. Williams can even echo the Apostle Paul's insight that "whenever I am weak, then I am strong" (2 Corinthians 12:10) when he suggests that "people of great strength tend to have weaknesses as great as their strength (because our strengths and our weaknesses are in fact the same things)."[4] Even though Williams did not feel the need for faith, he could see that Dylan had the wisdom of weakness. That is, Dylan was honest enough to admit his weaknesses to God, and therein lay the strength of his Christian music.

When Williams talks about the music, he is an expert with a lover's ear. He points out, for example, the effective way that

Dylan sings to both God and his consort simultaneously on the songs "Precious Angel" and "Covenant Woman." He hears how a song like "What Can I Do for You" is as simple and sincere as "Blowin' in the Wind." He observes that "Solid Rock" has one of the finest bass-line hooks in the history of rock and roll. And he imagines that "In the Garden" reaches back to the mystery plays of the Middle Ages with its deliberate tempo and ponderous mood.

When Williams sets about explaining Dylan's conversion, rather than explicating the music, he is less persuasive. The thesis of Williams's book is that Dylan's conversion was the direct result of his disillusionment with women.[5] Furthermore, Williams argues, Dylan's disillusionment was of his own making, since he had invested so heavily in paying musical homage to the illusion of the all-powerful female figure. Williams helpfully traces the record of Dylan's stormy marriage to his first wife, Sara, throughout his songs of the seventies. When Dylan's marriage finally dissolved (they divorced in 1977) and Dylan realized that there was no way to regain what he had lost, he had to face the void. Others have made this claim as well, though none quite as starkly as Michael Gray: "This is the pivotal theme of all Dylan's major work of the 1970s. Dylan's journey is from Sara to Jesus."[6] Williams begrudgingly admits that there were other factors involved, most notably Dylan's experience of Christ as an objective and mysterious presence in his life. Nonetheless, he insists on reducing Dylan's spiritual life to a soap opera melodrama about a man who could not keep his sexual longings to himself. And his tone is condescending. When Dylan reached the end of his rope, Williams writes, "He found the discipline he needed to save himself in an American cultural ritual called giving oneself to Christ."[7] Dylan's story is reduced to a stereotype.

Besides the pop psychology, Williams's explanation fails because Dylan did not give up his idealization of women after his conversion. There is no evidence of such a shift in his music until "Love Sick" from *Time Out of Mind* (1997), and even that song displays ambivalence about women rather than a deep-seated change of attitude: "I'm sick of love but I'm in the thick of it / This kind of love I'm so sick of it." In fact, if *Slow Train Coming* does anything to his attitude to women, it consummates it. In his early work, Dylan often sought the divine in the feminine, a quest that is bound to end, as Williams argues, in disillusionment. But Williams is wrong to think that Christianity simply replaces the love of women with the love of Christ. Faith organizes human desires so that believers can love all things in the proper way—as God loves them. Thus, "Precious Angel" shows how Dylan was finally able to see the feminine in the light of the divine, rather than the divine in the light of the feminine. This powerful song is born of gratitude to the woman who led him to Christ. That gratitude is erotic because Dylan's newfound faith has awakened the whole range of his emotional life. Many critics were turned off by this song's attitude toward his "so-called friends," who told him about every religious figure except "the Man who came and died a criminal's death." They are being too hard on him. Dylan is not gratuitously dumping old friends. Instead, he is drawing a contrast between those who had "fallen under a spell" and the "sister" who could show him "how weak was the foundation I was standing upon." Dylan is able to sing "Shine your light, shine your light on me" with conviction because he knows that his "sister" is not God, even though he comes close to merging her identity with the divine in the opening lines, "Precious angel, under the sun / How was I to know you'd be the one." Rather, she is part of God's plan. While many of his earlier love songs seemed confused about the precise status of a woman's sacred hold on him, this one can go all out in celebrating his woman friend because he knows she has led him to a greater good. His love for women has been redeemed.

The relationship between secular and sacred love is further clarified in "Covenant Woman" from *Saved* (1980). Dylan has a covenant with her just as she has a covenant with God, and the two covenants are mutually reinforcing. She is "shining like a morning star," but Dylan adds, significantly, "I know I can trust you to stay where you are." What is remarkable about these lines is not the clichéd image of a beloved shining like a star but the way Dylan qualifies that image. Precisely because she shines like a star, with borrowed light, Dylan knows that she is not going to compete with the sun/Son in his life. She will stay right where she is, but this is not a put-down. She is way up in the sky, in a position of brilliance and beauty, yet she need not be put higher than she deserves. Only when Dylan turns his eyes to God can he put women in their proper perspective.

Williams is right that Dylan's attitude about women, as expressed in his songs, changes, but the changes are a result of his conversion, rather than a cause of it. Dylan is able to write a different kind of love song after his conversion because his love of God brings new order to his other loves. Ideas, not inner psychic dramas, drive Dylan's musical changes. Dylan has always been rightly disturbed by armchair psychological speculations about his lyrics because, like all great artists, his music is about much more than his personal life. If his songs were merely commentary on his love life, they would not be so powerful.

Knowing a little bit about Dylan's life is helpful in coming to understand his music, but the key to his music has to be found within the music itself. His evolution as an artist is driven not only by ideas but also by his investment in sound. Consider some of his comments about sound in various interviews. In 1965, when he went electric, he declared, "They can boo till the end of time. I know that the music is real, more real than the boos." In 1975, in the midst of marital problems, he said, "There is a voice inside us all that talks only to us. We have to be able to hear that voice." And in 1978, just before his conversion, he mused about his earliest recordings, "I have to get back to the sound that will bring it all through me."[8] As great as he is, Dylan's genius does not lie in abstract philosophizing. He finds meaning in the music, and that is where we have to look to find out what he means to us.

That is where we have to look to find out what he believes about God as well. The simplest explanation for Dylan's spiritual conversion is that a musical trope became a living reality. He was always drawn to the gospel sound, but at some point, he began inhabiting that sound rather than merely playing with it. Dylan's musical interest in Jesus goes back to the beginning of his career. Before his twentieth birthday, he had sung Woody Guthrie's "Jesus Christ" and the traditional "Jesus Met the Woman at the Well." In 1962, he wrote "Long Ago, Far Away," which opens and concludes with the death of Jesus. The first stanza is poignant:

> To preach of peace and brotherhood
> Oh, what might be the cost!
> A man he did it long ago
> And they hung him on a cross
> Long ago, far away
> These things don't happen
> No more, nowadays.

Dylan evidently was not a Christian at the time, but his song certainly was!

For whatever reason, Dylan was long haunted by the story of Jesus Christ. The most remarkable evidence of this is on the unreleased "Sign on the Cross" from the Big Pink basement tapes. The sign the song refers to is the one under which Jesus was crucified. It declared, mockingly, that Jesus was "The King of the Jews." Dylan is asking in this song if that is true. The refrain goes, "And it's that ol' sign on the cross / That worries me." The sign on the cross, the song continues, is the key to the kingdom. The song begins like a traditional hymn with a country flavor and, before a concluding stanza, moves into a spoken monologue that can only be called a sermon.

> Ev'ry day, ev'ry night, see the sign on the cross just layin' up on top of the hill. Yes, we thought it might have disappeared long ago, but I'm here to tell you, friends, that I'm afraid its lyin' there still . . . the sign on the cross is the thing you might need most.

Some critics have heard in this song a tongue-in-cheek oddball fantasy, with Dylan playing the theatrical role of an old-time preacher. It is true that the song is trying on an old-fashioned musical style, but the words are too powerful to be a put-on. Dylan is struggling for a form to express his ambivalence, perhaps even his confusion, about faith. Dylan is worried, not converted, but where does conversion begin, except with a question that starts to worry you?

One should not get the idea that Dylan's interest in Christianity only coincided with his passion for old-ftime, primitive music. While the religious substance of *John Wesley Harding* (1968) is often acknowledged, the case can be made that *New Morning* (1970) is even more immersed in religion. This is the hardest of all Dylan albums to classify, and it was not a commercial success. It anticipates Dylan's gospel music by using a female chorus and putting Dylan at the piano. Religious references abound, but one song sticks out theologically. "Father of Night" is a simple prayer to God that could have come out of a nineteenth-century hymnal.

Closer to the time of his conversion is the movie *Renaldo & Clara*, produced as a kind of farcical document of the Rolling Thunder Revue (1975–76). Many Dylan watchers tie the failure of this project to his conversion, though there is no hard evidence for that little bit of speculation. The idea that Dylan was falling apart in the seventies and that the film exhausted his energy, making him vulnerable to Christianity, cannot be passed off even as a slight exaggeration of the facts. It is a fantasy—an attempt to lay a narrative grid on Dylan's complex life with little confirming evidence from Dylan himself. What *is* interesting about the film is that it is suffused with Christian imagery. At one point, for example, the camera dwells on some carvings of angels on a church. This is hard to describe or put in context, because the film's plot is very dreamlike. Moreover, the sound quality of the only available edition of the film—a bootleg of a German television broadcast; Dylan pulled the film from American distribution soon after its release and has never made it commercially available since—is terrible. Nevertheless, at one point in the film you can hear everyone singing, perhaps on a bus, a song that Dylan seems to have written. It comes out of nowhere and doesn't go anywhere, but it stuck with me. The words are simple:

> Tell me what will you do when Jesus comes.
> Tell me what will you do when Jesus comes.
> Will you tear out your hair?
> Will you sit down in your chair?
> Tell me what will you do when Jesus comes.

The song goes on to ask, "Will you kick him in the street? Will you drive him in the heat?" Although the Rolling Thunder Revue appeared to be full of drugs and sex as well as some great rock and roll, this is not the song of a man uninterested in religion.

Street Legal fared little better than Dylan's movie. It was recorded and released in 1978, his last album before his conversion. Again, for those who want to see Dylan's conversion as the result of his decline and fall, this album functions as little more than another misstep on his way down to the religious gutter. The album was mainly criticized for its poor production quality. Always looking for the authentic sound that was captured on his earliest records, Dylan decided to make the record at his rehearsal studio in Santa Monica, in a building that used to be a gun factory. The result demonstrated that Dylan's desire for a spontaneous, immediate sound was no longer something easily contrived. Studio technology had become so sophisticated that it picked up every little noise, making it nearly impossible to play live and have it recorded right. The live sound has to be carefully manufactured and, even then, it does not sound the same as it used to.

Nevertheless, there are some great songs on the album, and several of them have religious themes. For example, the backup singers to "New Pony" sing an unsettling refrain in a gospel style with the words "How much longer?" The most powerful song on this album, "Señor (Tales of Yankee Power)," can be heard, in retrospect, as a harbinger of Dylan's conversion. It is addressed to a mysterious señor who seems to have the answers Dylan is looking for.

> Señor, señor, do you know where we're headin'?
> Lincoln County Road or Armageddon?
> Seems like I been down this way before
> Is there any truth in that, señor?

The subtitle of the song has misled some critics to scrutinize it for a political message about the plight of Hispanics. On the contrary, the song is heartbreaking in its plea for help. Dylan asks the señor (Spanish for lord) to "disconnect these cables [and] overturn these tables," an allusion to Christ's overturning the money-exchange tables in the Temple. By asking him to disconnect the cables, Dylan not only accomplishes a sly internal rhyme but also draws a parallel between the moneychangers and his own musical career. He is weary with the musical business. "I'm ready when you are, señor," he sings. Other lines on this album also stand out when they are viewed with the hindsight of Dylan's conversion: "Go down to the river, babe / Honey, I will meet you there," "I'm exiled, you can't convert me," and this wonderfully obscure stanza from "Where Are You Tonight? (Journey Through Dark Heat)":

> The truth was obscure, too profound and too pure
> To live it you have to explode
> In that last hour of need, we entirely agreed
> Sacrifice was the code of the road.

Curiously, that song begins with a reference to a long-distance train rolling through the rain. Dylan had been on the road for some time, but that road was about to end at a slow train coming around the bend.

Dylan was not the only one in his crowd to start thinking about where the road was taking them. Some of the musicians on Dylan's tour, including T-Bone Burnett, became born again in 1976, and a few of them had the nerve to talk to Dylan about their newfound faith. Dylan's next major tour, in 1978, was a more subdued affair. Being on the road for a year gave Dylan plenty of time for sexual affairs, and several of his girlfriends—Mary Alice Artes, Helene Springs, and Carolyn Dennis—came from the gospel tradition and were Christians. Artes introduced him to a small but growing evangelical church known as the Vineyard Fellowship in January 1979.

Vineyard was founded by Kenn Gulliksen in 1974. When Dylan's conversion became public, the media invariably referred to this church as fundamentalist. This was a misconception. Journalists did not know how to distinguish evangelicalism, with its emphasis on personal testimony and religious experience, from fundamentalism, which was much more concerned with biblical literalism and strict morality. Even today, many people have little idea about the way evangelical churches have succeeded in blending popular culture and Christian worship, with enormous growth as the result. California led the way in using rock on Sunday mornings, and the Vineyard Fellowship was right on the cutting edge. While mainline Protestant churches were watering down their doctrine and moving to the political left, evangelical churches were combining a hard-hitting sound with straight-talking theology. Dylan spent more than three months taking weekday morning classes on the Bible at the Vineyard Fellowship.

To be more specific, the media disseminated one basic misunderstanding of the Vineyard Fellowship. It was portrayed as a kind of cult, brainwashing Dylan among others. This is understandable, since the media typically conceives of any kind of religious passion as intolerant, and the invitation of salvation as a demand for converts to give up their past identity. In fact, the Vineyard did not push the gospel as a hard sell, nor did it ask Jews, for example, to give up their Judaism in order to become Christians. Many people attracted to the Vineyard Fellowship were Jewish, and they actually became more Jewish when they became Christian. Like many evangelical churches, the Vineyard emphasized Christianity's connection to Judaism and treated authentic Judaism as compatible with Christian faith in Jesus the Messiah.[9]

Even before he started attending church, Dylan had several experiences that led him down the garden path. At a November 1978 concert, someone threw a silver cross onto the stage. Dylan picked it up and kept it. He was not feeling too well and decided he needed the extra help. Then, in a Tucson hotel room, he had a direct experience of Jesus Christ as Lord of Lords and King of Kings. As he told Karen Hughes in an interview in 1980, "Jesus put his hand on me. It was a physical thing. I felt it. I felt it all over me. I felt my whole body tremble. The glory of the Lord knocked me down and picked me up."[10] The visionary had discovered what he had long been dreaming about.

In the same interview, he made two exceedingly dry observations. First, he cynically noted—years before George W. Bush answered the question about his favorite philosopher—that politicians talk about God in general but "none of them are speaking about being a disciple of Christ." When Dylan became religious, he did not want to be religious in general. He wanted to be grounded in a specific revelation of the divine. Second, he wearily observed that it would have been a lot easier if he had become "a Buddhist, or a Scientologist, or if I had gone to Sing Sing." Perhaps because Christianity is so influential in America, it is held to higher standards than any other religion or ideology. It is easier for a rock star to admit a drug addiction and enter rehabilitation than it is to confess a spiritual transformation and join a church.

Enumerating the spiteful and condescending remarks made in the media about Dylan's Christian music would take too long and be too depressing. Most of the criticisms were so hostile that they seemed like invitations to a hanging. However, one group's reaction was understandable. Dylan had rarely spoken out about his Jewish upbringing, but many Jews counted him as one of their own. Dylan's most Jewish song, "Forever Young" from *Planet Waves* (1974), which was said to have been written for his youngest son, echoes the parents' Blessing of the Children on Shabbat. Dylan was photographed visiting Israel on his thirtieth birthday, and there were rumors before his conversion to Christianity that he was investigating his Jewish heritage. Whenever a Jew—any Jew—converts to Christianity, many in the Jewish community cringe. Dylan's conversion made the Jewish community sick. Looking back on it, Nadine Epstein and Rebecca Frankel state, "Not since Shabbatai Tzvi's 17th-century about-face did an exit from Judaism shock the tribe like Dylan's Christian period."[11] The reference is to a charismatic Jewish teacher who was identified by some as the messiah but ended up converting to Islam.

Jews felt betrayed, and everyone else was befuddled. Perhaps one quote is enough to give some of the flavor of the media responses. Greil Marcus is one of the most astute followers of Dylan's musical journey, and he has written profoundly about the weird, old America that lies behind Dylan's music.

Nonetheless, when Dylan converted, Marcus simply could not get it. "Listening to the new Bob Dylan album [*Slow Train Coming*] is something like being accosted in an airport."[12] The Christian faith was beyond Marcus's auditory horizon.

Marcus was playing the role of the sophisticated defender of high culture who was ordered to protect the gullible public by turning off Dylan's lowbrow sound. The distinction between fine and popular art often hangs on the twin criteria of complexity and originality, criteria usually associated with texts, not music. Music that does not "read" with all the ambiguity of a written text is thus dismissed as simplistic and sentimental. Likewise, words that come from a shared oral tradition, where no individual takes credit for authorship, are considered less original than words penned by a single individual. Marcus knows better than anyone how unfair these criteria can be. Black gospel music, for example, can be deeply complex in vocal development and emotional effect while utilizing fairly simple and unoriginal lyrics. Marcus understands how subcultures submerged in American history achieved aesthetic impact through direct emotional appeal and communal standards of meaning rather than from intellectual subtlety, but he was not willing to grant such status to the evangelical lyrics Dylan was now singing.

Evangelical Christianity is a complex subculture because it began in a position of dominance and then went underground. Nearly all Christians were evangelical in the nineteenth century, and evangelicals were engaged in the entire spectrum of social and political causes. After the rise of Darwinian science and the historical criticism of the Bible, however, a great silence descended upon evangelical Christianity in the early part of the twentieth century. By the seventies, this sleeping giant was about to be rocked awake.

The term *evangelical* is hard to define and has undergone some subtle changes of tone, but basically it refers to devout Christians who seek to spread their faith. When the Roman

Catholic Church broke apart during the Reformation and the Enlightenment began the slow, painful process of partitioning reason from faith, Christians were confronted with two basic options about how to adapt to the modern world. They could compromise by accommodating theological beliefs to the spirit of the day (the liberal option), or they could try to retain their traditions by renewing them through revival (the evangelical option). Both adaptations work, but different places and times render one or the other more or less successful. Evangelical modes of adaptation are just as dynamic and creative as liberal modes, even though evangelicals are often stereotyped as being behind the times.

Actually, drawing attention to the distinction between liberals and evangelicals is a bit misleading, since most Protestant Christians since the Reformation have been evangelical. Only a small minority of the cultural elite have tried to attenuate Christian claims to meet the intellectual needs of the ruling classes. The influence of these theological claims adjustors, especially in higher education, is so out of proportion to their numbers that they have been able to rewrite Christian history as a story that climaxes with their own ascendancy to the upper echelons of the American elite. Liberal historians identify their ideological peers as the agents of progressive social change. In reality, evangelical Christians were the most politically active in the nineteenth century, shaping public discourse about slavery, temperance, voting, child labor laws, and most other reforms. Only when evangelicals lost local control of schools—both public and private, due in part to the controversy over evolution—did they go into hiding from public debates. They were not idle in their seclusion. Instead, they were busy building a vibrant subculture and awaiting their opportunity to emerge into full view, since they never lost faith in America as an essentially Christian nation and never gave up their suspicion that liberals were stretching faith to the breaking point. Their political hibernation came to an end when

Reagan made his pact with the religious right, and their political viability at the polls was assured by their growing alliance with Roman Catholics, who were once their theological enemies. Evangelicals were returning to their activist roots, but they had been politically dormant for so long that many liberal Americans were shocked and confused by their insistence that they had the right to be politically involved.

Dylan's Christian concerts were one of the first seismic tremors to alert the proper cultural authorities to the emergence of a previously submerged subculture into the mainstream. The debates that quickly erupted about *Slow Train Coming*, therefore, had little to do with the actual music, which was astonishing. Producer Jerry Wexler gave the album the smooth bluesy sound of black soul music, and Mark Knopfler of Dire Straits gave it a syrupy guitar tone that was sweet if a bit thick. The result was a huge commercial success, and many critics agreed it was the best-sounding album Dylan ever recorded. Dylan won the first Grammy of his career for "Gotta Serve Somebody." Jann Wenner, editor of *Rolling Stone*, assigned himself two pages in his own magazine to rave about Dylan's achievement. "Musically," he concluded, "this is probably Dylan's finest record." Nonetheless, many of Dylan's most avid fans kept booing, as if they had to punish Dylan for devoting the best production qualities of his career to promulgating the Christian faith.

Even Williams, for all the musical compliments in *Bob Dylan—What Happened?*, pushes himself to the front of the pack of journalistic hounds hungry to bite their master. Since Williams is relatively careful with his theological criticisms, he can provide a good case study of the problems much of the media had (and still has) in thinking about the aesthetics of Christianity. For Williams, the problems with Dylan's theology are plain. While once he was on the side of the political good guys, "Now he has or seems to have joined up with the forces of sexual repression, mindless nationalism, and religious intolerance."[13]

Williams goes astray when he separates the substance of Dylan's message (which he does not like) from its acoustical form (which he does like). This is bad critical practice in any circumstance, but it is especially regrettable concerning *Slow Train Coming*. Of all of Dylan's albums, this one most perfectly marries substance and form. The music simply *is* evangelical, and the words could not be other than they are. Just try to imagine Dylan singing something more theologically agreeable to the pulsing drums and the soaring guitar work on this album. How could he moderate his imperative, "you're gonna have to serve somebody," without making it a farce? How could he suggest that none of us is perfect without simply saying that "ain't no man righteous, no not one"? How could he take out the references to spiritual warfare and still have words that keep up with the beat? How could he ask us to wake up in a softer voice and still make it rock and roll?

Williams's reservations about Dylan's theology are little better than stereotypes. His criticisms can be put in three broad categories: Dylan's theological exclusivity, the lack of a progressive social program in his lyrics, and Dylan's alleged anger. Williams was not alone in being offended by Dylan's exclusivity, but he was one of the few critics who had a sense of humor about it. He confesses that he is not "necessarily very far from loving Jesus right now. But I'll be damned (ahem) if I'll enter into a monogamous relationship with Him."[14] Williams is put off by Christian exclusivity because he does not want to leave out a large part of humankind from his relationship to God. He is worried about, in a word, intolerance. He says all of this as if it were an obvious objection to an evangelical style of faith, but his own metaphor of marriage suggests that there might be something more to religious exclusivity than intolerance. Religions make ultimate demands on their followers, and those demands are transformative only when they are understood to be singular and unique. Religious pluralism—the idea that all religions are roughly equal in theological value and ethical content—may work well in theory, but is hard to sustain in practice. In fact, monotheism has always been a demanding faith, in all of its historical trajectories (Judaism, Christianity, and Islam). Faith in one true God entails the recognition and rejection of false gods. That is what gives monotheism its social relevance and its transformative power. Exclusivity also enables monotheism to imagine the transformation of the entire world, since only a God who made everything can change everything as well. Exclusivity has its religious benefits as well as its cultural drawbacks.

Tolerance is an important value, but making it an absolute does little good for anybody. Tolerance, in fact, provides little leverage for social critique. Prophets cannot be tolerant, for example. There is a time for qualification, but there is also a time for exclamation. The problem is that some liberals are so committed to freedom of expression that they have difficulty in hearing, or making, criticisms of the moral decline of modern culture. Schools remain on safe ground by teaching tolerance, which is often the only moral virtue they teach, because tolerance is so easy to promulgate in the framework of moral relativism. Nobody is challenged, because everything is okay. Of course, tolerance is secretly insidious, because teachers can use it to threaten those whose convictions cross the rhetorical line of moderation and consensus. Tolerance does have a critical component, then, but instead of interrogating society, it excludes the most overt criticisms of the status quo.

Dylan was aware of these problems with tolerance long before criticisms of political correctness began to emerge in countercultural media outlets. Critics rarely pay attention to his frequent analyses of the devil, but his theology of evil is a complex and profound response to the social valorization of tolerance. Satan, for Dylan, does not come in the guise of moral vices. Instead, Satan is the voice that tells us everything is okay. Satan seduces us through perversions of the good, rather than promoting what we already know is bad for us. "Trouble in Mind" from *Slow Train Coming* brilliantly conveys the way that Satan can "deaden your conscience 'til you worship the work of your own hands." The good has a hold on us, through our conscience, which is why we can always rationalize our tendency to use what is good for our own selfish purposes. Sex, for example, is good. Its goodness, not its badness, is the source of temptation. If it were not good, it would not hold out so many false promises for us. "Satan will give you a little taste, then he'll move in with rapid speed," Dylan sings in "Trouble in Mind." Dylan reinforces this analysis when he confesses, in "Ain't No Man Righteous, No Not One," that he has "Done so many evil things in the name of love, it's a crying shame / I never did see no fire that could put out a flame." Far from preaching hellfire and brimstone, Dylan is telling us that when we love wrongly, we love the right things in the wrong way. Loving harder will not set things straight. When we love for misguided reasons, more love only makes matters worse.

Dylan's most insightful commentary on evil can be found in "Man of Peace," which is on *Infidels* (1983). He paints a scene of someone at a window, listening to a band playing Dixie and looking at an outstretched hand. The hand "Could be the Führer / Could be the local priest." Dylan is daringly suggesting not only that Satan is a man of peace but also that true religion brings a sword, not a peace sign. No rock-and-roll song has ever been so incisive about the way, as Dylan states in this song, "Good intentions can be evil." The bluntness of that line should not be taken as a sign that the song lacks subtlety. Dylan is at his rhyming best when he sings, "Well, he can be fascinating, he can be dull / He can ride down Niagara in the barrels of your skull." The image of Satan taking a joy ride in the tumult of one's brain is slick and scary. Dylan probes even deeper when he states, "He's a great humanitarian, he's a great philanthropist / He knows just where to touch you, honey, and how you like to be kissed." Again, Satan tempts us by offering us more of the good than we have a right to claim. We can think we are being generous when we are really being foolish, manipulative, promiscuous, or worse.

Dylan put his theology of sin into practice in one of the most controversial episodes of his career. In 1985, Dylan appeared at the end of the Live Aid benefit show, which reached an estimated two billion viewers. The concert served the noble cause of raising money for starving Ethiopians. There were technical difficulties, and Dylan was not at his musical best. Yet the critics thought that his words, not his sound, needed adjusting. Dylan took advantage of his position to draw attention to the plight of American farmers! He was either acting the fool or he was speaking wisdom that went way over the heads of his audience. True, American farmers were going through a very difficult period, but many people thought he was drawing a moral equivalence between American farmers and Ethiopians. Clinton Heylin, for example, says that Dylan missed "the distinction between someone struggling and someone starving."[15] If Dylan was doing that, he was worse than a fool. His remarks did inspire Willie Nelson's Farm Aid benefits, but his moral analysis can stand on its own. Dylan was musing out loud about the way in which the wealthy—and rock stars are very wealthy—use their resources to further their self-image, rather than to solve social problems. It is easier to love someone who is little more than an abstraction than to take care of those who are in your own backyard. Loving your neighbor is more demanding than loving those who live far away in exotic lands. As Dylan told Anthony Scaduto, "You can't go around criticizing something you're not a part of and hope to make it better. It ain't gonna work."[16] Doing good deeds for those who are some other government's problem is commendable, but you can lose your soul in the process, since these good deeds are too easily turned into symbols that do little more than reflect the egos of the do-gooders.

Secular liberals want to help everyone, but true hospitality, Dylan seems to be saying, involves some element of exclusion. If you try to love everyone, you end up loving nobody. The hardest (and most important) person to love is the one you are with right now. Having said this, it is important to point out that Dylan's religious exclusivity on *Slow Train Coming* has been crudely exaggerated. The opening song, "Gotta Serve Somebody," is a tour de force of inclusivity, not exclusivity. Dylan levels the spiritual playing field by including everyone, even himself, in his critique. The line "You may be a preacher with your spiritual pride" puts Dylan—and all Christians—on spiritual trial. The repetition of "You may be" is democracy in sonic action. Moreover, "you're gonna have to serve somebody" is hardly a rigid proclamation. Anybody listening to this song can relate to it, religious or not, because, on its surface, it states an obvious fact. Yet maybe the offended were right in their reaction. The song is prescriptive, not descriptive. Dylan does not say that everyone does serve somebody, whether he or she likes it or not. This is not another "Maggie's Farm," where Dylan protests against involuntary labor. Dylan projects servitude into the future in this song. At some point in time, you will have to decide whom you want to serve. In case anyone doesn't understand this, Dylan puts plenty of menace in his voice to underline his meaning.

Williams decries the exclusivity implied by "Gotta Serve Somebody," but that exclusivity is the foundation for a new wave of social criticism that eclipses Dylan's protests from the sixties. That claim should not be surprising. From which perspective is a more total critique of the status quo likely to come: confidence in the redistributive power of the government or fear of God's final judgment? Take, for example, "When You Gonna Wake Up?" This song is more specific in its target and clearer about its intentions than anything Dylan wrote in the sixties. "The rich seduce the poor and the old are seduced by the young," he sings, adding a slam against "pornography in the schools." Many critics have been baffled about this reference to pornography in the schools. Williams wonders what he means by it and whether porn is really a significant social problem. Anyone who has had kids in public schools needs no explanation of Dylan's complaint. Young girls are taught by popular culture to look more and more like sexual toys and the rock world itself rarely rises above the image of girls as instruments of male pleasure.

In "Gonna Change My Way of Thinking," Dylan confesses his own need for a new set of moral rules. The second stanza observes that it is becoming hard to keep track of all of the oppression in the world. Dylan then proceeds to overturn our perception of what oppression is. Rather than talk about the easy examples of victimized minority groups, he holds up sexual disorder, as with "old men turning young daughters into whores." Given all the reports of Dylan's womanizing and the confessional context of this line, Dylan is admitting his involvement in the problem. But he is honest enough to see that there is a serious problem in America culture with the sexualization of adolescent (and even preadolescent) girls.

Dylan continues his critique of the unexpected in "When You Gonna Wake Up?," which targets the "instant inner peace" promised by New Age spiritual gurus. When Eastern religions are exported to America, they easily become part of a spiritual marketplace that seeks to satisfy quick consumer demand. They lose anything that does not promote positive thinking, including their metaphysics, their history, their rituals, and their dogmas. They become "counterfeit philosophies" that pollute, rather than cleanse, our thoughts. This is social criticism at its most pointed, because it wounds the vanity of those who think they have transcended the stifling spiritual conformity of the Christian masses.

Protest music is angry, and anger is the hardest emotion for a Christian to express in a loving way. Since Christianity preaches so strongly against spiritual pride and hypocrisy, Christian anger can seem self-serving rather than socially transformative. You can think you are being critical of the ways of the world when in reality you are merely being proud of your own special knowledge. Only God can love in anger. Sin taints human anger with resentment and hate, whether it is hatred toward others or self-hatred. Nonetheless, anger can serve a useful social function, even though it is almost always corrosive when it becomes too much a part of one's personal life. Dylan's anger in his Christian music has been much maligned, as if this were a new mood in his work. Williams, for example, complains about Dylan's angry tone, but he also realizes that Dylan is up to his old tricks. In fact, Dylan is trickier than ever. In relation to his Christian songs, "Like a Rolling Stone" is easy to handle because Dylan's venom is striking someone else. The audience is on the singer's side, while somebody else takes the fall. The fact that the subject of the song is an unnamed woman allows the audience lots of imaginary space to play out its meaning. In the Christian songs, his listeners are the target. There is nowhere to hide.

Dylan made his Christian music to create discomfort, and he succeeded. Williams protests, "I want to make a strong distinction between helping people to search their own hearts versus asking them to stand up and be counted."[17] The distinction is duly noted by Dylan, who has no interest in the former and every investment in the latter. Williams assumes that people are wise enough to conduct a search of their own hearts objectively, and that their hearts are receptive to being searched. Dylan assumes otherwise, as he made clear in a 1985 interview with Bill Flanagan. "Most people walking around have this strange conception that they're born good, that they're really good people—but the *world* has just made a mess out of their lives. I have another point of view."[18] What Williams does not see is that the tone of justice in evangelical theology is, more often than not, one of righteous anger rather than optimistic idealism (although evangelicals certainly do not have a monopoly on such anger). Besides, Dylan does not neglect humor on *Slow Train Coming*, most notably with the reggae-infused quasi-children's song, "Man Gave Names to all of the Animals," which ends abruptly with the appearance of the snake.[19]

Slow Train Coming is a masterful summation of evangelical theology. Every scrap of sound on the album is intentional, and the intention is to create a sense of urgency about witnessing for Christ. Evangelical Christianity was always the functional equivalent of rock music in the Christian world. Evangelicalism emerged out of nineteenth-century revivals, and being loud and unruly is as essential to revivals as it is to rock concerts. Crucial to evangelical Christianity is a sense of an impending doom that forces you to make a decision. Dylan had long been singing about the end of the world. Now he knew how it was going to end and what we should do about it.

Many of his earliest classics were meteorological meditations on the end of the world. In these storm songs, he contemplated the symbolism of total closure with an intensity that has not been heard again in contemporary music. Just a list of Dylan's apocalyptic songs conjures up a mood that is as enduring as it is difficult to describe: "Blowin' in the Wind" (1962), "A Hard Rain's A-Gonna Fall" (1962), "When the Ship Comes In" (1963), "The Times They Are A-Changin' (1963), "Chimes of Freedom" (1964), "Gates of Eden" (1964), "It's All Over Now, Baby Blue" (1964), "Desolation Row" (1965), "Visions of Johanna" (1965), and "All Along the Watchtower" (1967). These songs evoked the rain, but his music did not bring on the flood until *Slow Train Coming*.

Slow Train Coming provides the key to Dylan's dark, apocalyptic mood in the sixties. In fact, he was already using the symbol of a slow train back in 1965 on the liner notes for *Highway 61 Revisited*. The sixties were explosive, but Dylan's music envisioned a closure to history that was hardly in tune with the progressive utopian pacifism espoused by the peace movement. Because Dylan began writing apocalyptic songs when much of America was worried about the nuclear threat from the Soviet Union, his music could be interpreted as a political response to that situation. It is better understood as a much more fundamental exploration into time and its ending. Dylan uses the Soviet threat to articulate a set of concerns with a much longer history than the Cold War. It is God who is angry, not Russia.

From the beginning of his career, Dylan was a visionary in search of a sound that would do justice to his visions of justice and transformation. The justice he preached, however, was not the liberal kind of distributing wealth and leveling the playing field so that equality can leaven the disruptive effects of economic competition. He did not think people working for good causes could fundamentally change the world. In theological terms, the idea of the perfect world is called the kingdom of God, and the idea that the kingdom of God can be the byproduct of human effort is called postmillennialism. Postmillennialism teaches that Jesus Christ will not return to Earth until humans have at least tried to meet him halfway. That is, human effort, in cooperation with divine grace and guided by biblical principles, can go a long way toward achieving spiritual ideals on Earth before Christ returns to crown our efforts.

Postmillennialism was the dominant theology of the nineteenth century, which is why so many people then were involved in social reform movements, from abolition and temperance to child labor reform and women's right to vote. America was a thoroughly Protestant country buoyed by the hope that the New World could become the site of a radically new moral order. Musically speaking, postmillennialism is sentimental and mainstream, because postmillennialists believe that the seeds of utopia have already been planted by social reformers and need only the right bit of care and nourishment to bring forth their fruit. Postmillennialists are convinced that the future will keep getting better and better. The status quo needs correction, but we do not need to start all over with a clean slate, which would wipe out our virtues as well as our vices. Postmillennialism is a dominant tone in American music, with its optimism about the future and its confidence in the goodness of humanity. Nevertheless, postmillennial theology seems unreal to many people today, because few of us think that the best of human intentions can reshape society from the top to the bottom. Culturally and politically, postmillennialism is dormant, but the sound of postmillennialism, which is moralistic and earnest, still finds expression in much popular music.

The opposite of postmillennialism is premillennialism, which argues that the world will come to a terrible end before Christ establishes his reign of righteousness for all to see. The "pre" means that Jesus Christ will rescue (or rapture) the faithful before the tribulation begins and that only after this tribulation will Jesus establish his thousand-year reign. In other words, the world is going to get unimaginably worse before God makes it unimaginably better. Premillennialism emerges from a deep mistrust of human nature and an abiding alienation from the dominant trends of history. It suggests that people are blinded to their situation, since most people go along as if nothing dire is about to happen to them. Death is at the door not just for each one of us but for planet Earth as well. Premillennialism is the theology of the disenfranchised. Those who cannot place their trust in social and governmental institutions to save and protect them must look elsewhere. At its worst, premillennialism can give way to paranoia and misanthropy, both of which are present at times in Dylan's music. At its best, premillennialism gives meaningful shape to rage by putting desperation to song. Premillennialism has a Pentecostal and black sound. Nothing is held back, because the time is short. There are no qualifications, hesitations, or complications. The world is divided between the saved and the damned, and there is no middle ground.

Dylan was a premillennialist long before he became acquainted with Hal Lindsey's *Late Great Planet Earth,* the 1970 book that made premillennialism popular in America. It is nearly useless to speculate about the psychological and biographical sources of his interest in end-of-the-world theology. He was probably more attracted to the music than to the theology of premillennialism. Though they lack many of the cultural comforts of the elite, premillennialists have a lot of the best music. Urgency, anger, and pain intermingle with an unimaginable hope to produce sounds that are riotous and raging.

Dylan's sound has always been in the premillennialist style, which makes it surprising that his secular critics were so taken aback when he embraced the substance of premillennialism as well. What is even more surprising is the reaction of the churches to Dylan's music. Much of this chapter has been devoted to criticizing Dylan's secular critics. It would be wrong to end the chapter without admitting that the Christian music industry has also all but turned its back on Dylan's gospel songs. Contemporary Christian music has become big business, and most of it is bland, optimistic, and computer-driven. Even Christians with premillennialist beliefs listen to postmillennial music. Dylan's end-of-the-world sound was too much for even most Christians to appreciate.

Perhaps Dylan's music is just too individual to find a place with either Sunday morning praise bands or Christian radio. Dylan made rock and roll safe for many evangelicals, just as he once elevated rock to the level of art by infusing amplified music with the depth of the folk tradition. His Christian music is timeless, but it has failed to affect our time as much as it should have. Our popular culture, for better or worse, is in no small part coextensive with contemporary popular music, so it speaks volumes that Dylan's musical sermons are still blowing in the wind.

Notes

1. Wayne Hampton, *Guerilla Minstrels: John Lennon, Joe Hill, Woody Guthrie, Bob Dylan* (Knoxville: University of Tennessee Press, 1988), p. 191.

2. The entirety of *Bob Dylan—What Happened?*, which is out of print, is contained in *Bob Dylan: Watching the River Flow, Observations on His Art-in-Progress, 1966–1995* (New York: Omnibus Press, 1996), which is a collection of Paul Williams's writings.

3. Paul Williams, *Bob Dylan: Watching the River Flow*, p. 96.

4. Ibid., p. 115.

5. Later, after talking to one of Dylan's closest friends, Williams revised his thesis to emphasize the role of mortality in Dylan's conversion. See Paul Williams, "Bob Dylan and Death," in Bauldie, ed., *Wanted Man: In Search of Bob Dylan.*

6. Michael Gray, *Song and Dance Man III: The Art of Bob Dylan* (New York: Continuum, 2001), p. 213.

7. Williams, *Watching the River Flow*, p. 102.

8. *Younger Than That Now*, pp. 67, 99, and 121.

9. For interviews with Vineyard pastor Bill Dwyer that make these points, see the Joel Gilbert documentary *Rolling Thunder and the Gospel Years: A Totally Unauthorized Documentary* (Highway 61 Entertainment Production, 2006).

10. Karen Hughes interview, Dayton, Ohio, May 21, 1980, originally printed in the New Zealand newspaper *The Dominion*, Aug. 2, 1980.

11. Nadine Epstein and Rebecca Frankel, "Bob Dylan: The Unauthorized Spiritual Biography," *Moment* (August 2005), p. 81.

12. Greil Marcus, "Amazing Chutzpah," *New West* 24 (Sept. 1979), reprinted in *The Dylan Companion*, ed. Elizabeth Thomson and David Gutman (New York: Dell, 1990), p. 237.

13. Williams, *Watching the River Flow*, p. 129.

14. Ibid., p. 104.

15. Heylin, *Behind the Shades Revisited*, p. 581.

16. Scaduto, *Bob Dylan*, pp. 176–77.

17. Williams, *Watching the River Flow*, p. 112.

18. Bill Flanagan, *Written in My Soul: Rock's Great Songwriters Talk about Creating Their Music* (Chicago: Contemporary Books, 1986), p. 104.

19. For a really brilliant reading of this song, which makes the case not only for its profundity but also for the idea that its abrupt unwillingness to name the snake is tantamount to a defense of the purity and creativity of the human word, see Ruvik Danieli and Anat Biletzki, "We Call It a Snake: Dylan Reclaims the Creative Word," in *Bob Dylan and Philosophy*, ed. Peter Vernezze and Carl J. Porter (Chicago: Open Court, 2006), pp. 90–99.

CHAPTER FOUR

A "Voice You Could Scour a Skillet With"

ob Dylan was born in 1941, early enough to witness the birth of rock and roll, but by the time he was a teenager, Elvis Presley had been drafted into the army and was no longer doing his thing. Rock, so soon after its birth, had entered a period of decadence and decay. Radio stations imposed a three-minute limit that reduced the basic song format to a formulaic melodrama. Dylan had heard Buddy Holly play the National Guard Armory in Duluth in 1959, just days before Holly was killed in a plane crash. Dylan would later recall how he sat near the front, and how Holly looked right at him. Holly was an original, but in his wake, rock was becoming derivative and schmaltzy. Americans were eager to listen to the radio while they ate, drank, and drove, but as a result, the music, like the food and the cars, had to be easy and fast. The music Dylan loved—the dissonant, Christ-saturated, stubbornly independent, holy rolling all-American sound—was driven into the bohemian underground.

Dylan enjoyed the excessive lifestyle in Greenwich Village in the early sixties, but he was a bohemian in spirit, not substance. In a revealing passage in *Chronicles*, he conveys his ambivalence about the sixties' obsession with personal freedom in a provocative meditation on the legendary civil rights anthem "We Shall Overcome." That song, he suggests, delivers more than the sentiment of protest; it summarizes the philosophy of a generation bloated on narcissistic dreams. "The dominant myth of the day seemed to be that anybody could do anything, even go to the moon." That sounds great in theory, Dylan admits, but he goes on to list the absurd consequences of a society that pretends to abolish all limits: if you are a housewife, you can become a glamour girl; if you are slow-witted, you can become a genius; and if you are old, you can become young again. "If you were an indecisive person," he jokes, "you could become a leader and wear lederhosen." This offbeat comment is meant to remind us that lurking behind the façade of anxious self-invention is an authoritarian personality: if you think you can remake yourself from scratch, what is to stop you from thinking that you can remake the world as well? Capitalism tries to soothe our inward emptiness with a multiplication of choices to meet every mood, but that only exacerbates modernity's crisis of self-identity. The sixties saw human nature treated as a malleable material for experimentation and recreation. In retrospect, says Dylan, "It was almost like a war against the self."[1]

Dylan could sound like he was at war with himself, and his voice broke all kinds of sound barriers, but he had a respect for tradition that defied the libertine spirit of the day. As inventive as he was, Dylan was always paying homage to the past. To take one example, he tried to live up to the primitive originality of Robert Johnson, the King of the Delta Blues, who had recorded some powerful songs in the thirties before disappearing into the

Mississippi haze. Even more influential was the rural sound of Woody Guthrie, whom Dylan began imitating while still in Minnesota. When Dylan finally met Guthrie in a VA hospital in New Jersey, Guthrie could barely speak. Huntington's chorea made Guthrie slur, ramble, and huff his way through his words. He had to breathe hard to utter a single syllable. Guthrie's wife "was convinced that these young guys were picking up these early Huntington's symptoms. . . . Holding a note and then kind of trailing [off], which was really a lack of control. That became the style [and] the jumping off point for Dylan."[2] Whether this bit of speculation holds any truth, it is fascinating to think of Dylan learning from a hospital bed how to fill words with the sound of a dying man's last breath.

Even when Dylan's voice sounds ghostly, he keeps it steadfastly earthbound. When he was growing up in Hibbing, Minnesota, the mass media had not yet flattened the musical landscape. The various regions of America sounded different. The live music Dylan heard on Saturday nights, for example, was polka, and it was played fast and loud. Radio stations preserved the uniqueness of weird and wonderful musical idioms like ragtime, Delta blues, gospel, hillbilly, and Appalachian folk. It was easy to imagine that these kinds of music were close to the way people actually lived their lives. To a teenager in a small midwestern town, every song could seem like its own species, revealing a strange new animal in need of inspection and examination. Radio was more than background noise. The airwaves were a spiritual medium, transmitting disembodied voices in all of their sacramental mystery. The atmosphere crackled with the "ghost of 'lectricity" that Dylan sings about in "Visions of Johanna."

Regional radio broadcasts sharpened Dylan's sense of hearing. Television is a highly centralized medium that tends to standardize public speech, so it is fortunate that TV was still in its infancy when Dylan was a teenager. Radio not only preserves the natural variations of the human voice, it also requires more auditory imagination than television. The radio concentrates all of the senses on sound alone. When television supplanted radio, sound was reduced to accompanying sight, and sight became the primary sense. Audiences became viewers, not hearers. People wanted to see action when they heard someone talking. Consequently, public speaking lost much of its social status. This is why students get bored when they have to listen to a lecture, and even popular music, which does much to perpetuate the prominence of the human voice, surrounds the lyrics of a song with a deafening drone of jangled noise.

In the days of Dylan's youth, sound carried more ontological weight than sight, which is just the reverse of today. Instead of watching TV at night, people often sat on their porches and listened to the sounds of nature, an exercise in attentiveness that evolution had pressed hard into the human psyche. Before Edison's invention, you would hear someone approach in the dark before you saw him or her. Visitors had to clear a path with their voices and turn their walk into a greeting. Voices were both wilder and more natural than they are today. They also were louder and stronger back then—just read any account of an open-air meeting prior to the twentieth century, whether it was religious, political, or theatrical, and you will marvel at the descriptions of vocal dexterity and auditory stamina. Speakers put more of themselves into their voices, and audiences were more willing to work their ears to detect the subtleties of human sound.[3]

Dylan had just enough of one foot in the old world of acoustics to bring it into contact with the new world of amplification. Coming of age during this pivotal point in the history of sound, he learned how to channel voices from the past to disturb the deaf and wake the dead. The result, needless to say, was explosive—to be more exact, the result was the explosion we call rock and roll.

To be honest, much of the power of Dylan's voice can be attributed to the way he works against the genre of rock. Like television, rock has had a negative impact on the way we hear and understand the human voice. Rock was not content with the relationship between instrumentation and vocalization that dominated popular music prior to the sixties. In pop songs, the voice leads up front. The instruments dutifully follow. In rock, by contrast, instruments converge to simulate the motion and energy of chaos, so that many sounds are simply unidentifiable. It is hard to talk about rock music in any precise way because it is hard to distinguish the elements of the sound for the purpose of analysis and evaluation. Rock wants to thwart the ear's urge to tie every noise to an identifiable source.

Rock tends to submerge the human voice in anxious guitar work and an overheated beat. Drums beg to be banged, which forces guitars to be strummed harder. Instruments made for the electric age can be cranked, but the human voice, even when it is expertly amplified, strains to keep up. By necessity, vocalization takes on all the qualities of an electric instrument. This is one reason why rock lyrics typically range from the superficial to the obscure, rarely rising to the level of poetry. The pressure on the voice to keep up with the speed and power of the drumming and strumming renders the meaning of the lyrics largely irrelevant. It is no accident that the best rock songs are catchy phrases that can be chanted like mantras. Amid the noise, the human voice strains toward repetition and simplification, or veers into the nonhuman altogether.

John Lennon is thought to have been the first musician to record feedback on a record ("I Feel Fine" in 1964).[4] This seismic shift in acoustics has taught all of us to take pleasure in industrialized noise that probes the outer limits of harmonization. Before distortion, rock was already a rebellion against traditional forms of music. After distortion, rock became an assault on the very nature of hearing. At its best, distortion tries to encapsulate the experience of alienated teenagers on the verge of psychological disintegration. At its worst, distortion demonstrates the essentially narcissistic nature of most rock guitar playing, where sound circulates in a loop of self-indulgent fascination.

Distortion makes the noise of urban congestion a kind of constant background blare in much rock music. The singer gets lost in the crowd of busy street sounds. Voices have to be loud to be heard—or at least need to be subjected to various technological manipulations in order to complement the surrounding soundscape of a crowd on the move. In his interview with Cameron Crowe included in *Biograph*, Dylan laments, "I can see where pretty soon the human voice will be synthesized, become totally unreal. You know, like put in Paul Anka and get him sounding like Howlin' Wolf or vice versa."[5] Modern technology tries to dominate, rather than stimulate, the auditory imagination.

Even Dylan had to work hard to discover how he could maintain his vocal integrity in the midst of piercing guitars. Few singers can overpower the amps of a rock band, but Dylan could pull off the trick of making his voice as angry and abrasive as the slash of a guitar string, with offbeat diction to do battle with the drums. Dylan, in fact, worked against his vocal limitations in order to do battle with his backup bands. He turned his vocal weaknesses into strengths, foregoing the temptation to use the recording studio to enhance his idiosyncrasies. His diction in the sixties mixed the surrealism of beat poetry with the hard twang of a hillbilly cowboy to make a sound that was simultaneously sophisticated and coarse. It was too original to be pinned down by any musical genre.

Dylan's songs are, in a way, about his voice, but his songs are definitely not pop. In most popular music, the singer's voice sounds natural, in the sense that it is in continuity with the harmony we hear in the voices around us, even if popular music takes that vocal harmony in an idealized direction. Dylan's voice makes such natural harmonies sound superficial and artificial. His voice is eerie, evoking the supernatural in an uncanny way.

Nonetheless, Dylan's voice is not divine. His singing, in fact, can be downright ineffective when he settles for one tonal range, although even that criticism must be qualified. Nobody has utilized monotone to better effect than Dylan on songs such as "Hard Rain." Dylan can explore more sonic terrain within a single note than other singers with greater range can explore in an octave. Dylan is at his best when it seems that he is not satisfied with how he is singing, so that every tone has alternative overtones built into it, and every serene musical moment is following by an unpredictable shift of direction. His voice becomes as elusive as his personality.

Dylan's voice can be as hard to describe as it is to listen to. He can sound flat and agile, fecund and disembodied at the same time. It has often been observed that some people listen to Dylan in spite of his voice and others because of it. Some just don't like Dylan's music, period. In a way, it takes a leap of faith to enter into Dylan's sound, but once you are there, it is a long way to get to the bottom of what makes him so deep. The eminent writer John Updike was one of those who just didn't get it when he first heard Dylan perform. A review he wrote of a 1964 Joan Baez concert shows one of America's greatest writers trying to come to terms with the end of the folk revival. Updike admits he has long been in love with Baez, but does not like the "musical leaflets called 'freedom songs.'" These songs, which reflect "a commendable social concern among the guitar-playing young, illustrate the hard truth that more goes into a folk song than liberal sentiments, today's newspapers, and a rhyming dictionary." It is not that Updike does not like protest music. Rather, liberal folk music simply cannot "hold the stage with the authentic songs of the enslaved Negro, the frontier ballads, or the foreign songs that compose the folksinger's classic repertoire." These comments offer contemporary insight into the decline of folk music, but Updike is not able to see how Dylan is doing something new. Updike is such a great writer that his description of Dylan is worth quoting in full:

> And, the unkindest cut of all, Miss Baez yielded the stage, with a delight all too evident, to a young man, Bob Dylan, in tattered jeans and a black jacket, three months on the far side of a haircut, whose voice you could scour a skillet with. Dylan is, of course, the current king of his raw young profession, possessed of ungainsayable energy and an affecting, if exacerbating, presence, and it must be acknowledged that his plangent strumming and bestial howling gave the Baez concert what vitality it had. Miss Baez, this admirer was pained to observe, visibly lit up with love-light when he came onto the stage, and even tried to force her way, in duet, through some of the impenetrable lyrics that Dylan composes as abundantly as poison ivy puts forth leaves.[6]

In this revealing snapshot of a turning point in musical history, Updike puts his finest literary voice on display, as if he were trying to compete with the new musical fashion. Yet Updike, the most elegant of American writers and the epitome of *New Yorker* prose, could not see beyond Dylan's ruffled stage presence.

Then again, many people have preferred a cleaned-up version of Dylan's style rather than the raggedy real thing. To Dylan's credit, his songs have a musical power that transcends his own renditions of them. Covers of his work, which inevitably smooth the contours of his gritty intonations, frequently outsell the original versions. These imitations are evidence of the beauty of Dylan's melodies. While other performers try to isolate and enhance that beauty, Dylan tarnishes and smudges his melodies to create a more complex art. One of the secrets of his music is the tension he sets up between the melody and his voice. Rather than going along with the main current of the tune, he fights it. Dylan enjoyed going to jazz clubs when he first moved to New York. Charlie Parker was dead, but be-bop was still very much alive. Dylan's voice can be jazzy in the way it bops around the melody line in a restless and impulsive fashion, alternately staying ahead and lagging behind the beat.

Much has been made of Dylan's vocal confidence. He is aware of it: "You can do anything with your voice if you put your mind to it."[7] He came to New York fresh-eyed but broke, and he cut his first album in 1962 at the age of 20. On his debut album, Dylan sounds like an old man, and many of the songs (only two were originals) are obsessed with death and sacrifice. Dylan sings the old spirituals, "In My Time of Dyin'," "Gospel Plow," and "Man of Constant Sorrow," as if he were bringing them back from the Appalachian Mountains for the first (and last) time. The mystery of how Dylan could sound so old when he was so young has led to many forced explanations. One of his first girlfriends, Bonnie Beecher, has told the story of how Dylan contracted bronchitis in 1960, which, she claims, gave him his prematurely aged sound.[8] It seems easier to believe that he was born with an old soul than that he took advantage of damaged vocal cords.

All the songs on his next album, *The Freewheelin' Bob Dylan*, which was recorded the next year, were his own. With this work, he began driving a wedge between those who like his lyrics but not his voice and those who like both. The lyrics are powerful enough to be given both softer and rougher performances, and some people will always prefer the pretty to the profound. A cult-like atmosphere grew up around those who found the meaning not just in the words but in the way Dylan sang them. They could play his records repeatedly and feel that each time the songs sounded unique.

To perform in this manner took a lot of courage, but boldness alone could not create such mystery and intrigue. Voices are commanding because they disclose something of what a person hides within. A clue to Dylan's voice that is often overlooked is his longtime battle with stage fright. Most biographies of Dylan mention this phobia in passing, but none dwells on it, perhaps because Dylan himself never talks about it. The Band's "Stage-fright," written by Robbie Robertson and released on the 1970 album with that name, is said to have been "a little poke at Bob."[9] Dylan is a nervous performer and, even in his best concerts, he can take several songs to get into a comfortable groove. He is a private and introverted man who makes his living baring his soul. People who have battled stage fright talk about the immense struggle that takes place when they are suddenly thrust into the spotlight. This is only speculation, but it is not implausible to wonder if Dylan's vocal confidence has been won through intense psychological struggle. Some singers have a natural relationship to their voices, but Dylan is self-conscious about his. He changes his vocal style from album to album, and even within a single song, he is capable of making swift vocal adaptations. This is a man who thinks deeply about his voice and has turned that self-consciousness into art. More than that, Dylan's voice sounds wounded. As he sings on "Tomorrow Is a Long Time," "I can't speak the sounds that show no pain." His vocal vulnerability surely comes from battles deep within the dark nights of his soul. Stage fright might be one of the scenes of those battles. If so, what we hear in his music is the triumph of his vocal will overcoming his doubt and anguish.

Regardless of the source, Dylan's voice is enigmatic. Many of his fans obsess over the obscure details of his private life in the hope of discovering the secret of his art. This is a futile quest. No amount of gossip can lead to a deeper experience of the quality of Dylan's voice because Dylan's enigma is inherent in his music; it is not a riddle that can be solved by adding together various pieces of insider information. The enigma of Dylan's music is none other than the way it both calls attention to itself and generates a strained distance between performer and listener. Rock music usually tries to provide immediate satisfaction. Built into Dylan's music is a deep ambivalence about the pleasures of listening. He might have been inspired to embrace ambivalence in his art by the riled and erratic songs of Kurt Weill and Bertolt Brecht, which he heard early in his stay in New York City. Brecht created a theater of alienation, where actors hold the audience at arm's length in order to open up a space for forced reflection rather than instantaneous response. Brecht thought art should be hard. That is, art should repulse rather than seduce. Dylan took Brecht to heart. He does not want to make it easy for you to hear what he has to say.

One way to make hearing hard is to mumble, and much has been made, both positive and negative, about Dylan's penchant for mumbling, though it has rarely been analyzed in any depth. When Dylan was a teenager, his favorite movie star was James Dean, another great mumbler, who was surely the source of Dylan's cultivation of that trait. Dean played awkward young men who did not say much but exuded sincerity. Dean's mumbling was part of his rebelling. Likewise, Dylan's mumbling was designed to provoke, but his target was the folk revival. One of the chief aesthetic standards of folksinging was the clear enunciation of the words. Pete Seeger has said recently that he got mad at Dylan at the Newport Folk Festival in 1965 not because Dylan went electric but because no one could understand what Dylan was saying.[10] Folk music was message music, and to deliver a message, people had to understand what you were saying.

Mumbling can both put people off and draw people in. You have to lean in close to someone who insistently speaks in a soft, low, or faltering voice. Mumbling is protective and revealing at the same time. It can make the speaker look vulnerable and helpless, causing the listener to want to help finish the words. Mumbling, then, is a deceptive exercise of vocal power. By mumbling, Dylan takes words beyond their rational effect, but he does not leave words behind. That is, his mumbling does not end in chanting, wherein the sheer hypnotic force of the sound totally overwhelms the meaning of the words. Dylan is too much of a preacher to let that happen. He has something to say. He is not just communing through sound. His words carry the music as much as the music pushes the words.

Along with mumbling, Dylan distorts his voice in a way that can be likened to the literary trope of hyperbole, or exaggeration. Dylan got his start in coffee houses in Greenwich Village, where people were noisy and tourists would come and go, looking for the latest authentic representative of folk music. He told tall tales about himself to reporters in those early years, and his voice was also full of parody, wit, and make-believe. His eccentric phrasing and elongated syllables were, in a way, a parody of the hillbilly sound that had enchanted him back in Minnesota. Some of those who saw his first performances compared him to Charlie Chaplin. He poked fun at himself, made faces, and constantly wore a corduroy cap that he would fiddle with on stage. He had an abundance of nervous energy that came out in his body as well as his voice. To experiment with his voice and to test the limits of his range, he used exaggerated features of the folk and hillbilly traditions.[11] All singers exaggerate aspects of their natural vocal tone to achieve specific effects, but what set Dylan apart was the fearlessness of his ability to make his voice go wherever the lyrics took him. He exaggerates his voice to the point of changing it altogether. Dylan is the great hyperbolist of song.

The most obvious form that his exaggeration takes is a guttural quality that is hard to describe. In part, it can be attributed to his upbringing in a community dominated by immigrants, many of whom hailed from Germanic lands. People elongated and hardened their vowels, which could be heard most noticeably in the way they said "yar" for "yeah."[12] Interestingly, philosophers were once interested in the way vowels and consonants relate to meaning and the forces of civilization. The Greeks thought that any people who spoke with a growling tone were barbarians. To be civilized was to speak clearly, putting plenty of space between words and, for men, keeping your voice out of its lower reach. The nineteenth-century German philosopher Hegel, who loved the Greeks, argued that the vowel is "the pure sounding of the voice."[13] He did not mean this as a compliment. Consonants interrupt vowels and are the means by which humans construct meaning out of sound. Vowels are easy; consonants are hard. Consonants chop at sound, breaking it up into sharp pieces. The consonant is the sonic equivalent of the power of thought. Animals can make vowels, Hegel argued, while only humans can break up the fluidity of speech and transform sound into thought. Hegel is the greatest of speculative philosophers, and so his thought is as hard to understand as it is to apply to practical problems. But his suggestion that human meaning emerges in a kind of war between consonants and vowels can help explain the power of Dylan's voice. There is something both animal-like and sublime in many of Dylan's vocal performances. His vowels come from within a passionate place that speaks of ancient times. He is patient with letting his vowels find their consonants. He lets the sound of his voice work its meaning before analytical thought is allowed on the scene.

Nonetheless, Dylan is not all animal passion. On the contrary, he wants to make you think, while most rock stars want to make you dance. Thinking is hard work, which is why most people resist it, especially when they are listening to music. Dancing can be an appropriate response to music, of course, and it is, in a way, what much popular music "means." The best music, however, should elevate the mind as well as stimulate the body. Rock wants to deafen you to the voice of your conscience so that your body can be freed from the nagging reminder that you have a purpose higher than sexual frenzy. Rock washes over us with sound waves that give us a momentary thrill with little inherent meaning. We no longer have the patience to listen to music intended to move us spiritually. We do not know how to listen as if the future of our salvation were at stake.

Every culture, as well as every religion, gives sound a different shape, but some emphasize the tonality of sound over its vocative qualities. Some Eastern religions, in fact, portray the sound of mantras as more powerful than the gods themselves. For these traditions, sound is a means of inciting ecstasy and thus blurring the boundaries that separate people from each other. Dance is thus the most appropriate response to music. In dancing, the impersonal forces that hold sway over our lives are endowed with a sexual power. Rock music today is a return to these pagan roots. Idolatrous music prohibits all questioning. Christianity, by contrast, follows Judaism in introducing the question of truth to the phenomenon of sound. Christians believe that human beings are created to be hearers of God's Word. Consequently, we should never be satisfied with the beat and the noise. Music should be met with a decision about what it means rather than (or in addition to) a dance. Dylan stands in that heritage. He sings to your soul, and his songs demand an answer.

The biblical understanding of the spirituality of sound is thus crucial to any interpretation of Dylan's work. The monotheistic faiths of Judaism, Christianity, and Islam grant the human voice enormous power because God is the origin of speech. The God of the Bible is the One who spoke the world into being, commissioned the prophets to speak on his behalf, and became the living Word in Jesus Christ. We can speak because God has spoken us, and because God has spoken to us, speech is a holy thing. That is why the Protestant tradition elevates preaching to a central religious category. Nature too can praise God, and instruments can sing their own tunes, but we are only truly free when we find our own voices. And nobody has been more at one with his voice than Jesus Christ. The Gospels do not tell us what

Jesus looked like, but they describe the way he mesmerized the crowds with his parables. When Jesus worked his miracle with Lazarus, he showed that his voice could stir the dead. No wonder the Gospel of John reports the Temple police saying, "Never has anyone spoken like this!" (7:46).

Dylan's voice is the closest many of us have come to a contemporary analogue to the purely creative power of God's voice. Dylan awakens new levels of auditory responses as if he were waking the dead. How he does this is hard to describe. His voice can begin down in the ground and go high into his head, reverberating in his nasal passages and hiding in his throat. It is a voice that is always telling a story rather than aiming at a perfect pitch. It has all the contours of a body—all the weight of physical reality. It is textured to the point where it is touchable. Just when you think you have comprehended a line, he wrings another twist of sound, puffing out a final breath where others would inhale. How and when he breathes is an enduring mystery. Listening to Dylan is an auditory workout. Your ears are on full alert.

Dylan's sound can be pure, as it is on *Nashville Skyline* (1969), which can bewilder people when they hear it for the first time. *John Wesley Harding* (1968), his previous album, is austere and foreboding, but *Nashville Skyline* contains the sound of redemption. Anthony Scaduto has pointed out that many of Dylan's listeners, who associated country music with the "redneck" values of God and country, interpreted this album as further evidence of Dylan's growing political conservativism. As Stephen Scobie has observed, in a bit of understatement, "*Nashville Skyline* was not the album you wanted to listen to as you shipped out to Vietnam."[14] At least one critic thought Dylan was practicing the subterfuge of reaching out to the white working class in order to bring them into radical politics![15] This sixties revolutionary applauded Dylan's strategy of using a sincere and irony-free language in order to radicalize the masses by meeting them on their own level. Leftists could not believe what they were hearing, so they had to make up theories to explain away the evidence of their ears.

Vocally, *Nashville Skyline* is a leap forward in Dylan's range. There is no nasal entrapment or menacing whine in the tonal quality of his voice. Perhaps jokingly, Dylan attributed the change in his voice to his success in kicking the cigarette habit. Speaking to the simple verities of life, *Nashville Skyline* was a major commercial success, but it did not score on the country charts, even though it opens with a beautiful duet with Johnny Cash, "Girl from the North Country." Dylan was being too hip for country, just as this album was too country for the truly hip. He was also defying categorization by lifting his voice to the tenor range, which made him sound every bit as mysterious and eccentric as Roy Orbison. This album helped put Nashville on the rock-and-roll map and led the way to a new fusion of country and rock, but it might have been too happy for the kind of stories country songs were telling at the time. By not reaching deep into the country audience, it anticipated Dylan's groundbreaking Christian albums, which also were musical revolutions that failed to find a permanent home with their intended audience.

For the most part, Dylan's sound is rarely pure in a wholesome way, but its roughness does achieve what can only be called a kind of spiritual clarity. Dylan takes the low road to the palace of wisdom—which in America is a well-traveled path. In America, singing, like believing, was severed from the high culture of its European roots after the Revolutionary War. Music and theology were both democratized; the masses got a chance to raise their voices in song and sermon. Culture came down from the aristocratic elite to become incarnate in the most humble forms of human flesh. Dylan, who probably knows more about the roots of American music than any living performer, often sings as if he is exploring the democratic origins of American sound. Part of that exploration is attending to the christological shape of much American music. Early on, Dylan learned how to infuse his voice with the sorrow of Christian suffering. Critics who do not know the gospel musical tradition often miss this dimension of Dylan's voice. His cries of dereliction have become even more aching as Dylan ages and his voice becomes more vulnerable, to the point of being almost too painful to hear.

Dylan's voice has weight and density; it is substantial enough to connect soul to soul. Its textured surface makes it multidimensional, because the ear can discern its various layers, which get deeper with each hearing. Most rock songs go by quickly, but the palpable quality of Dylan's voice enables him to play with space as well as time, creating the acoustical illusion of a sonic equivalent to shades of color and shadows of light. He works his voice as potters mold clay. He can squeeze it, pinch it, and harden it, all the while shaping it into abstract designs. At times it is so guttural that it seems as if Dylan can lengthen his throat into a long tunnel of reverberation. He can also pitch his sound high through his long nose as if he were throwing his voice to someone else.

Much of the folk music that was popular during Dylan's youth had a homely sound. It was assuring, simple, and sincere. Joan Baez sounded radical because she brought a lyrical beauty to the folk tradition that transcended the genre. Her pure soprano voice was ineffable, even mystical, sublimating desire into religious purity. She called Dylan her "little vagabond" when she invited him to tour with her in 1963.[16] Vocally, she and Dylan were heading in the opposite direction, which must have doomed their romantic association from the beginning. Politically, they were never on the same page either. He was as prosaic as Baez was idealistic. "I asked him what made us different," she wrote in her autobiography, "and he said it was simple, that I thought I could change things, and he knew that no one could."[17] She eventually put her disappointment to music in the song "To Bobby," where she protested, "You left us marching on the road / And said how heavy was the load."

This is not to suggest that Dylan did not learn from Baez or benefit from their partnership. In the liner notes he wrote for *Joan Baez in Concert, Part 2* (1963), he mused about how she had helped him overcome his prejudice against conventional notions of beauty. Growing up, he writes, he found beauty only in the "ugliness" of railroad lines, cracked curbs, and clothes dusty with grime. When he first heard Baez play, he hated her sound. "The only beauty's ugly, man / The crackin' shakin' breakin' sounds 're / The only beauty I understand." Baez helped him to see that beauty could be found in more than the muck. Dylan put this lesson into practice most tellingly on "Lay, Lady, Lay," which he croons in the tradition of Bing Crosby or Frank Sinatra. What is fascinating is not how beautiful this song is but how much Dylan never really liked it. He thought it was not representative of what he does best. As much as he grew to appreciate Baez's talent, he was never really convinced that beauty could be found in idealizations of concrete reality.

"Lay, Lady, Lay" is a moving song, but Dylan is right that it is not indicative of his vocal identity. People who do not like Dylan's voice often really like "Lay, Lady, Lay." The obverse holds true as well. Those who like Dylan's vocal eccentricities can be very condescending toward the song. What both groups sometimes miss is the way Dylan's singing style was carefully constructed for a specific purpose. Dylan sang roughly because he wanted to express something essential about the American experience.

Dylan picked up some of his vocal mannerisms from Harry Smith's *Anthology of American Folk Music*, which he began listening to in 1959. First released in 1952, the *Anthology* was, in the words of Greil Marcus, "the founding document of the American folk revival."[18] Smith drew on his own collection of old 78s to put together a compilation of previously released songs from the twenties and thirties that were already old-fashioned when first recorded. The artists had stopped recording after the Depression and had been forgotten after World War II. The collection opened up a time warp to a new world of sound. Although Smith's parents were theosophists and his own views of religion and history were confusing and confused, his *Anthology* documented an acoustical battle straight out of the Beatitudes: the impoverished turning the tables on the privileged in order to gain a degree of cultural control over their lives. Much of the language of the songs came straight from the Bible, which was the only book many of the singers and their communities would have known. For the rural poor, religion was equal parts protest and consolation, but it is the protest that comes out strongest in the anthology. The performers caught on this record sang as hard as they lived. The vocals were honest rather than beautiful, but they were so true to their aim that they focused hearing as much as any great work of art arrests the eye. Their aim was to put emotion—usually pain and sorrow, but sometimes the unspeakable joy that comes from love, both religious and sexual—into song, and that aim became Dylan's as well. The music has had such a hold on Dylan that he came back to it in two acoustic albums, *Good as I Been to You* (1992) and *World Gone Wrong* (1993), and echoes of it can be heard on *"Love and Theft"* (2001).

Folk songs are often thought of as sincere, while Dylan's voice is usually considered authentic, but spelling out the difference between sincerity and authenticity is not easy. Sincerity, for example, does not do justice to the songs on Smith's *Anthology*. There are varieties of sincerity, but the one that comes to mind when that word is associated with folk music is the simple request to be trusted. People who are sincere sometimes lack confidence in themselves. They put their faith in the person beseeched. The overly sincere want to be believed so much that they are willing to sacrifice their own beliefs. Most of the singers that Smith recorded were not trying to please anybody, so they can hardly be considered sincere in that sense. Clearly, neither can Dylan. Rather than trying to persuade you to believe what he is saying, Dylan is trying to convince you to be suspicious of yourself. Dylan trusts himself, not his audience. He is authentic, not sincere.

Perhaps the best way to understand this difference is to compare Dylan's original recording of "Blowin' in the Wind" with the version popularized by Peter, Paul and Mary. Their version is sincere, which is why it, and not Dylan's, was a hit. People trust their voices because they do not demand anything from their audience. They are assuring, while Dylan is beguiling. In the Peter, Paul and Mary version, the questions are sung by different combinations of vocalists, but it is always Mary, gently and sweetly, who sings the "answer"—"The answer is blowin' in the wind"—as a solo. She turns the wind into a breeze. By doing so, she makes it sound as if there really is an answer, while in Dylan's version, it is fairly clear that there is no answer, or that, at the very least, a strong wind has blown it away.

The word *authentic* comes closer than *sincere* to describing the performers on Smith's *Anthology*, but even that observation needs to be carefully qualified. For something to be authentic, it has to be removed from the original to which it is trying to conform. The Smith artists simply *are* original; they cannot be measured by a truer tradition. The same cannot be said of fifties folksingers. If you are singing somebody else's words, or singing in a style not altogether your own, then you can be more or less authentic (or genuine) in your treatment of the material. In the folk world, with its dream of socialized property, there was always the question of whether the appropriation of someone else's labor was done out of the proper motives and with the right results. Fifties folksingers aimed at authenticity, by which they meant an accurate urban reprisal of old rural sounds.

How Dylan reinvents the notion of authenticity becomes clear when he is compared to folksingers. To return to the example of "Blowin' in the Wind," this classic song has obvious roots in traditional American music but, just as obviously, it is Dylan's own unique creation. It sounds like it could have been written decades before the sixties, but Dylan also gives it a contemporary stamp. The old joke that great poets steal while mediocre poets borrow is appropriate here. The truly authentic performer relies on the past without regret while stamping the tradition with his or her personality. Only dynamic traditions survive, and traditions become dynamic when their most loyal followers delve so deeply into them that they give birth to new aesthetic forms. The authentic singer is true to others by being true to his vision not of what the past "really was" but of what the past can still become.

Given his traditionalism *and* his ambition, Dylan easily could have become trapped between the alternative of either striving to reproduce the past or straining to be relevant to the present. What protected him from this trap was his sublime indifference to the effect of his communication. Dylan's indifference to his audience is sublime because it functions like a trap for the listener. Dylan does not ask to be liked, which might be a weakness in another performer, but he turns his negligence into the primary measure of authenticity. The authentic, in other words, becomes the *opposite* of the sincere, because the authentic asks for nothing. The authentic does not *need* to be trusted. It just needs to be expressed.

The way Dylan stole the concept of authenticity from the folk crowd and redefined it for the rock generation is best heard in "Like a Rolling Stone" from *Highway 61 Revisited* (1965). It is odd that, of all the love songs that Dylan wrote, this song of retribution is one of his most famous. If "Like a Rolling Stone" were merely about a young man venting his resentment against a former girlfriend, I doubt it would have had so much influence. What makes this song so wicked is the perversely broad semantic range of its anger. Dylan's tone is so fierce and personal that you do not want to get in his way, even though he gives you no place to hide. Dylan is taking something personally in this song, but it is not a fictitious girlfriend. Dylan is lashing out against the folk audience's expectation that he convey purified emotion through meaningful music. Instead of generating good vibes, he is interrogating the very nature of human emotion.

Dylan wrote this lover's fantasy of revenge in May 1965, after returning from a triumphant British tour. He was 24 and ready to quit. Everyone wanted something from him. Most demanding of all, his audiences wanted him to play his already classic folk hits exactly the way they were recorded. He needed space to develop his own performing style. "Like a Rolling Stone" slams against the musical industry's conventions that restricted the length, content, and diction of popular songs. The song is long, and Dylan's voice is menacing. If rock and roll doesn't get much better than this, it's because rock and roll cannot go much beyond a recording that captures the upper limit of defiance put to song. Rock is supposed to be explosive, but in this song, Dylan is standing awfully close to the fuse.

Dylan asks the girl of the song, "How does it feel?" The obvious needs to be emphasized: this is a rhetorical question. He does not need or want an answer. He is sublimely indifferent to how she feels. In the guise of a question, he is just "telling it like it is." He is daring not only the girl but also his listeners to answer the question, and he's gambling that no answer will be forthcoming. This song puts you, the listener, on the other side of your own feelings by erecting a barrier between where the girl of the song used to be and where she is now. She cannot understand where she is or how she got there. She does not know what to feel. That is where the song puts the listener as well. We are addressed by a question that silences us.

"Like a Rolling Stone" was a rebellion not only against folk music's confidence in the easy accessibility of emotional purity but also against the presumption of teenagers everywhere that they have a right to feel however they want to. It intimates that rage is more authentic than feeling "so fine" that you can throw the bums a dime. Dylan wrote the song when America was moving from the innocence of the early sixties to the disorder of the latter part of that decade. He captured an emotional state between the moral consensus the country was losing and the judgmental self-righteousness that was lurking on the horizon. It is tempting to read this song as an allegory of the sixties, but then we need to be reminded that the sixties were still unfolding when it was written. It was prophetic in anticipating the anger that the war in Vietnam would soon unleash, but it is important not to read the song in terms of events and attitudes that were still in the future in 1965. In fact, the song does not tell us how the singer feels about anything. The word "I" does not appear in the lyrics. We just know that the singer has knowledge that the victim of the song does not, and we can imagine that this knowledge was bought at a high emotional price.

Dylan is a master of the authentic, but the authentic is a hard ideal to sustain. Capturing a sound in the studio that is memorable without being trendy and personal without being sentimental or obscure is a dicey undertaking, which is why most rock albums are so quickly forgotten. Dylan recorded most of his albums live in the studio, with no overdubbing and little rehearsal. He wanted his songs to sound fresh and spontaneous. He could be careless in the studio, but only because his goal was not to "get it right," as if there were only one perfect form for each of his songs. He recorded to support his habit of performing, which is where the meaning of his music happens.[19] This quest for authentic sound served him well when recording studios were primitive and all he needed was his voice and some friends. This approach did not serve him well when his inspiration was blocked.

There is a thin line between the casual and almost accidental feel of an authentic performance and the disaster of an unplanned and uninspired recording session. Dylan has occasionally crossed this line. Nevertheless, he has persisted in his quest to live up to the sonic standards of his first seven albums, from *Bob Dylan* (1962) through *Blonde on Blonde* (1966). The sound on *Blonde on Blonde* was his richest to that point, layered and evocative, but it still had the straightforward feel of one person speaking in his own voice to some friends nearby. Recording technology would soon make that a hard feeling to reproduce. By the late sixties, many bands were pushing against the limits of technology in order to achieve more sophisticated and synthetic effects. The artificial was replacing the authentic. Dylan intentionally went in the other direction, with low-tech albums like *John Wesley Harding* and *Nashville Skyline*. Dylan tried to hold the middle ground between soft rock that was going sappy and hard rock that was all about amplification and its ramifications.

Singing was more of a calling than a joy ride for Dylan—more of a moral task than an occasion to party. No song he wrote captures the daunting nature of his art better than "Lay Down Your Weary Tune." This song was recorded as an outtake from the studio sessions for *The Times They Are A-Changin'* (1964), Dylan's third album. According to Dylan's biographer Robert Shelton, Dylan wrote it in autumn 1963 while staying at Joan Baez's cottage in Carmel Valley, California. In the notes he wrote for *Biograph* (1985), Dylan explains that the melody was influenced by an early Scottish ballad he had heard on an old 78 and could not get out of his head. The song also seems shaped by Dylan's proximity to Baez, since it has much of her serenity and composure. Dylan performed it for the first and last time at Carnegie Hall, October 26, 1963, two days after he recorded it.[20] The studio version was heard by collectors on bootlegs but was not officially released until the *Biograph* box set in 1985. The live version was finally released on *Bob Dylan Live at Carnegie Hall 1963* (2005). The Byrds recorded an ambitious version of it on *Turn! Turn! Turn!* (1966), but their harmonized treatment fails to bring out its timeless quality and does not do justice to its meditative tone.

Hearing it for the first time can be an astonishing experience. That it is not well known seems somehow fitting, since it sounds like it came from an ancient time and it descends upon your ears as if it could be the last song you will ever hear. In fact, it would only be understatement to call this song one of the most moving ever composed by an American. The qualification "by an American" is a touch of modesty added only because other countries have greater resources for combining sadness and joy in a single work of art. Americans tend to want their tragedy and comedy held apart as separate genres. In this tune, Dylan lets just a hint of joy arise from the sadness of the words, so that the sadness is not self-indulgent and the joy is not gratuitous. By bringing these two apparently conflicting emotions together in such inarguable perfection, he frees each of them to be experienced in their fullness.

There are three reasons—musical, philosophical, and theological—why this song alone is enough to take the measure of Dylan's genius. First, musically, Dylan's prematurely aged voice is a perfect match for the beguiling lyrics. His voice performs the metaphors he sings, becoming both the thing signified by his words and the signifier. That is, he lays down his voice, humbly and gently, thus embodying the meaning of the words in his performance. He does not overdo it, a temptation that would fell a lesser singer. To lay down your voice with such finality, you have to do it almost sweetly and lightly; otherwise, you would sound melodramatic. In this song, Dylan does not fly around the notes, buzzing at the melody as if the tune were beneath him. He lets the tune carry his voice, and he lets his voice bring the tune down at the end of each line to a settled (if unsettling) conclusion.

Second, philosophically, it is Dylan's most mature statement about the nature of sound. No other piece of rock music so deftly and powerfully interrogates the basis of its own existence. Dylan is a consummate performer, but writing with the unbelievable energy that kept the songs pouring out of him in the sixties must have been exhausting. It took a motorcycle accident in 1966 to force him to abandon his career for a few years and focus on his young family. This song anticipates that accident with its knowledge that the end must come. Although he had many years of productivity ahead of him, Dylan knew, at an early age, that his inspiration would come and go, since it was not under his command. He saw his songs as gifts, even though he did not always use the language of God and grace to conceptualize the gifted quality of his writing. He knew that the music came from a higher place and that it was meant to take you back to the place from whence it came. Music, however, can only take you so far. Songs can say that they are building a stairway to heaven, but they remain the stairway, not heaven. This song says the tune is coming to an end, but it cannot *be* the end it is slowly coming to.

And third, theologically, "Lay Down Your Weary Tune" is the missing piece to a complete picture of Dylan's apocalypticism. Much of Dylan's end-of-the-world sound is on the side of righteous judgment, but this is a highly personal and surprisingly consoling composition. Songs like "When He Returns" (1979) are more explicit in their focus on Christ as the climax of history, but they have an urgent feel, as if the music is trying to push God to speed up the divine timetable. "Lay Down Your Weary Tune" has Dylan bringing together in one sonic reflection his own personal demise with the ending of everything around him. Although it was written long before his Christian conversion, this song about the end of songs brings Dylan's theology to a full and concluding circle by turning apocalypticism inward. Substitute "life" for "tune" (for Dylan, songs were his life) and you will hear how Christian the song is. The singer of these words is not trying to change the world or pick an argument with anyone about how soon the world will be changed by God. He is talking to himself more than to anybody else. He has had to carry his tune like Jesus carried the cross, and it is time to put it down. In that regard, this is a song about self-sacrifice, because only by a final surrender can we hope to have everything restored.

Any one of these three reasons would make this song stand out in Dylan's oeuvre. Bring the three together and you have the most sublime song of America's most daring songwriter.

"Lay Down Your Weary Tune" sounds like a hymn and reads like poetry. Although Dylan is often called a poet, this is one of his few songs that can (and should) be read on its own, regardless of its musical setting. Its imagery weaves together a seamless cloth of sound by transferring the intentional action of manufactured instruments to the organic processes of nature's seasonal cycles. This song is often identified as Dylan's one great tribute to pantheism. According to this interpretation, the work expresses Dylan's vision of the immanence of God in nature, but no reading of Dylan's music has ever been more off the mark. What is most lovely about the lyrics is that they keep humanity in the center of the drama even while nature—and God—move in their mysterious ways. Dylan asks the listener to imagine new ways of hearing the sounds of nature, but the song is not suggesting that nature as such speaks to us with the voice of God. The point at which we will cease to sing corresponds to the moment when music will accompany us in a new key. If nature, not God, were the source of all sound, then our death really would be the beginning of silence and that silence would be terrifying. This song suggests that we need not fear death, because at that moment we will find that the tune we carry has really been carrying us all along.

"Lay Down Your Weary Tune" lets us hear what the end of the world will sound like. It asks us to pause in order to listen to what we would hear if we were not around to make any noise. The reason we can try to imagine what nature will sound like after we are gone is that God spoke nature into being with the same voice that saves us through Jesus Christ. The sound of nature transcends the noise we make because out of the silence God spoke through Jesus Christ.

There is much to remark upon in the opening stanza, which Christopher Ricks has depicted as a "tender pitying admonition that is sung with sweet solemnity."[21] Its alliterative fecundity makes its repetition (as every other stanza until the last two verses, which are linked without the repetition of the refrain) welcome and renewing. The message of the refrain needs reiterating, because it invites the listener to do the impossible.

> Lay down your weary tune, lay down
> Lay down the song you strum
> And rest yourself 'neath the strength of strings
> No voice can hope to hum.

Notice that the identity of the subject being addressed in the first line of the stanza is left ambiguous. The singer of the song could be addressing another singer, but since we are all singers of our life stories, the singer is more likely addressing everyone. But the singer also seems to be addressing himself. He is calling on himself to go quietly into that dark night. In other words, the singer is both the addressor and the addressee. Even that interpretation, however, is unsatisfying, because this song is too great to be a monologue. It makes more sense to imagine that the singer is entering into someone else's voice. That is, the singer is *being addressed* by someone else. He is giving voice to the way in which he is being called to meet the end. The singer is speaking for God.

Each line of the song is the story of creation in miniature, rising step-by-step only to be sonically lowered to the ground. After all, to "lay down" means to establish as well as to relinquish, as in laying down a line of poetry to accompany a tune. In the beginning, God says "let there be," but in the end, God asks us to let go, and our only choice is in how we respond. We can return to the dust from which we came defiantly or gently. If laying ourselves down were a form of giving up, this song could not be so peaceful. Our letting go is a creative act that does not create out of nothing—as God does in Genesis—but does give us hope that there will be something more to life when we are through.

The creative character of this letting go can be heard in the repetition of "lay down" at the end of the opening line, which lets Dylan's voice drop a little, heightening the effect of the words. Of course, Dylan cannot both sing the song and lay down the song that he is singing. He is putting into words something that transcends the possibilities of our understanding. Just as some philosophers argue that we cannot experience the moment of our death, this song captures the impossibility of knowing the moment when the world dies to be reborn. I say reborn because this song is as full of promise as it is expressive of the relief of a final and complete closure. The mixture of anticipation of the future and release from all worries is captured by the word "rest" in the third line. The third line, in fact, is a remarkable image precisely because it is impossible to imagine. The song asks the singer to lay down what he is strumming and rest beneath the strength of strings. But whose strings are these? No instrument is mentioned, because it is the song itself that is strummed, yet "strum" and "strings" imply something being played. Simply put, one cannot strum strings and lay beneath them at the same time. The explanation for this paradoxical image unfolds in the rest of the song, where we discover the ways in which nature becomes the sounds we try to play. Here is the rest of the song:

> Struck by the sounds before the sun
> I knew the night had gone
> The morning breeze like a bugle blew
> Against the drums of dawn

Lay down your weary tune, lay down
Lay down the song you strum
And rest yourself 'neath the strength of strings
No voice can hope to hum

The ocean wild like an organ played
The seaweed's wove its strands
The crashin' waves like cymbals clashed
Against the rocks and sands

Lay down your weary tune, lay down
Lay down the song you strum
And rest yourself 'neath the strength of strings
No voice can hope to hum

I stood unwound beneath the skies
And clouds unbound by laws
The cryin' rain like a trumpet sang
And asked for no applause

Lay down your weary tune, lay down
Lay down the song you strum
And rest yourself 'neath the strength of strings
No voice can hope to hum

The last of leaves fell from the trees
And clung to a new love's breast
The branches bare like a banjo played
To the winds that listened best

I gazed down in the river's mirror
And watched its winding strum
The water smooth ran like a hymn
And like a harp did hum

Lay down your weary tune, lay down
Lay down the song you strum
And rest yourself 'neath the strength of strings
No voice can hope to hum

The last line of the refrain is the pivotal point—the still, small voice—of this poem. Dylan prolongs the word "hope" with his voice, giving it extra syllables and infusing it with, in fact, hope. He is indicating the way that all singing seeks to be accompanied—by a voice that can sustain us at our lowest point. By beginning the line with "no," Dylan denotes the finality of death. By ending with "hum," however, he leaves the door open for rebirth. Moreover, this line divides perfectly into two metrically equivalent half lines, a division common in many of Dylan's lyrics. Each half line consists of three beats: "no voice can" and "hope to hum." The denial and the affirmation are perfectly tuned to each other.

Here we must take a brief detour from my analysis. Michael Gray is one of the most thorough and insightful critics of Dylan's music. More than anyone else, he has been responsible for igniting critical attention to this song-poem. He devotes a whole chapter to it in *Song and Dance Man III*, where he calls it "one of the greatest and most haunting creations in our language."[22] I agree. On a less positive note, he has also been responsible for the idea that this song is a paean to pantheism.[23] (Pantheism is the idea that nature contains the whole of God, rather than being a manifestation of God's power.) Even the astute literary critic Christopher Ricks thinks the song describes an eternal circle of nature that beseeches the singer to respond with stoical passivity rather than with Christian faith. Ricks bases his analysis on the idea that Dylan is dealing with the spiritual malaise of sloth in this song. From Ricks's perspective, Dylan is confronting the weariness of all performers that drags them down and thus tempts them to lay down their art, rather than the need of all humans to give in to death with hope. What connects the analyses of Gray and Ricks is the idea that final truth is to be found not in the human voice but in the sounds of nature.

The key to Gray's interpretation is the claim that the last line of the refrain leaves implicit a word that he makes explicit:

"No *human* voice can hope to hum." In other words, Grey thinks that this song is declaring that only nature can provide the strength that enables us to rest. He admits that it is implausible to think that this is the one and only song Dylan ever wrote with a strong bent toward Eastern mysticism, but he makes the argument anyway. He does not explain how the song could have so much power over us if its origin lay in a culture far, far away. Contrary to Gray, I want to argue that the song is shocking precisely because it is so hauntingly familiar. It has nothing exotic about it. I agree with Gray that it attributes voice to all of nature (although I would want to underscore the metaphorical nature of that attribution), but that means it is a glaring error to expand upon Dylan's taut line with the insertion of "human." Dylan meant what he said. No voice, human *or* earthly, can hope to hum the final strength we need. Rather, that voice belongs to the One who is both human and divine, Jesus Christ.

Gray further develops the case for pantheism by emphasizing the various interconnections among the elements of the song. He argues that the song, like nature itself, manifests a self-renewing structure. The repetition of the first stanza he takes to be a sign of the cyclical nature of the seasons and thus indicative of the Eastern understanding of the circular nature of time. The travesty of this reading is suggested by Gray's own comment that the song resembles a pilgrimage, which is a religious journey to a specific destination, not an anonymous immersion in the endless cycles of the seasons. "Lay Down Your Weary Tune" has the slow but steady pace of a determined passage. The pacing is established by an insistent strumming that never loses a beat. The result sounds like a death march, or a final voyage that the pilgrims do not want to end. Dylan's pacing is brilliant in its ability to create the effect of an ending that is both coming and postponed. He manages to encapsulate our ambivalence about finality in its purest form. The song does not want to end, even as it slowly struggles for acceptance of the end. Just as "Lay

Down Your Weary Tune" holds together sadness and joy, it holds together progression and delay. Never has musical progression felt so inevitable.

That Gray is stretching to make his case is further indicated by his farfetched references to drugs. He claims that this song demolishes all distinctions in the way that only a drug trip could explain. I will not go into his comparison of the song to a passage from J. R. R. Tolkein's *The Lord of the Rings*, since he seems unaware that Tolkein was a devout Roman Catholic. What is most sad about his fumbling with this poem is how he compares it to "what an LSD vision can offer."[24] In fact, he argues, "no other song could enforce, for me, so strong a sense of the acid-mystic equation's validity."[25] In other words, the purpose of this most sober of songs is to legitimate the sacred value of psyche-delics. Lest I be accused of stretching Gray's malleable interpre-tation out of any recognizable form, let his own words get right to the point. This work, he says, is "Dylan's first acid song."[26] Now, it is true that between the very beginning of Dylan's career and his turn toward a spare, understated style with *John Wesley Harding*, Dylan relied on a highly allusive style that was drawn from beat writers like Jack Kerouac and Allen Ginsberg. *Blonde on Blonde* contains songs that could be classified as "druggy," but what does that explain? Many of Dylan's lyrics could be highlighted in such a way as to fit Gray's category of an "acid song," though Dylan's use of intuitive associations and juxta-posed time frames can be traced to other influences as well. In the seventies, for example, he took painting lessons, which had a profound effect on his handling of temporal sequencing in his writing. In any case, in various interviews, Dylan has talked about marijuana being a part of the musician's scene, but he has denied ever being interested in psychedelics.[27]

Dylan did not need to drop acid to write this song. He just needed the Bible close by—and some old records. Gray com-pares this song to a performance by Rev. J. M. Gates, "Oh Death,

Where Is Thy Sting," which Dylan would have heard on Harry Smith's *Anthology of American Folk Music*. Gates (1885–1940) was one of the most recorded black artists of the early twentieth century. His sermons were musical, and his music was sermonic. In this particular speech-song, Gates belts some lines (slightly revised) from the hymn "I Heard the Voice of Jesus Say." That hymn was penned by the Scottish evangelist Horatius Bonar (1808–80) and has been often recorded. It begins, "I heard the voice of Jesus say / Come unto me and rest / Lay down thou weary one, lay down / Thy head upon his breast." The similarities to Dylan's song are apparent, from the repeated "lay down" to Dylan's reference to love's breast. Nevertheless, Gates's words are hard to make out and the selection on Smith's *Anthology* is very brief.

A more likely influence, which Gray does not identify, is a hymn written by Ira Sankey. Sankey (1840–1908) was a singer and songwriter who traveled with Dwight Moody, one of the most popular evangelists of the nineteenth century. His music powered Moody's preaching, which made Sankey nearly as well known as Moody. Sankey wrote a number of songs that find an echo in Dylan's work, including "A Shelter in the Time of Storm." Most of his hymns were composed to be sung at revivals, and this is the case with "The Christian's Good Night." Sarah Doudney (1841–1926), a prolific author in her own right, wrote the poem "Good Night" as a eulogy to a friend. Sankey set it to music and it became known as "The Christian's Good Night." The first stanza reads, "Lay down, my dear brother / Lay down and take your rest / Oh, won't you lay your head down / Upon your savior's breast." The laying down is clearly a reference to the lowering of a body into the grave. This song was widely recorded, and as tuned-in as Dylan was to gospel music, it is likely he heard at least one of its many versions. The Grateful Dead were so taken by this traditional melody that they often ended their concerts with their own a cappella version of it, "And We Bid You Good Night," which was a real crowd-pleaser.

"The Christian's Good Night" is an invitation to the afterlife that sounds almost like a lullaby. This song, and not drugs, is the ancestor of Dylan's masterpiece. "Lay Down Your Weary Tune" has nothing to do with drugs or pantheism. Instead, it is a sober valediction, bidding farewell to the world. It is important to note in this connection that Sankey was a veteran of the Civil War. Sankey's tune is haunted by that catastrophe, which forever put an end to American innocence. Americans learned to deal with the unbearable memories of the countless dead on the Civil War battlefields by infusing their sorrow into spirituals about the death of Jesus. Of course, no eulogies could do the war dead justice. The Civil War left nature itself mute with exhaustion, yet the survivors had to find some tune to hum. Dylan's song resonates with the music of the Civil War—a period that has always moved him—as in the image of a morning breeze blowing like a bugle "against the drums of dawn." The wind is a recurring motif in Dylan's music, and its symbolism is closely tied to the Holy Spirit. The breeze appears to be calling the battle drums to account. It almost seems as if the song is being sung by someone who has survived one of the great Civil War battles. The singer stands before the sun, but it is not the night that haunts him. It is the previous day, when the drums signaled the beginning of battle.

Besides the Civil War, Dylan's song also shares with "The Christian's Good Night" a thoroughly biblical worldview. To be more specific, the song's biblical cadence comes from four primary sources: the Psalms, the Apostle Paul, the Hebrew Prophets, and the Book of Revelation. First, the harp mentioned in the second-to-last stanza ("The water smooth ran like a hymn / And like a harp did hum") is a sure giveaway that Dylan is modeling his song on the Psalms. No single person is more associated with the harp than the biblical King David (though the instrument he played is probably more accurately called a lyre, the ancestor of the modern harp). This harp that did hum provides a clue to the unnamed instrument—the one with strong strings—alluded to in the refrain. Dylan's silence about what this instrument is probably leaves the impression in many minds that Dylan is talking about a guitar. Dylan does strum a guitar throughout the song, but whoever heard of resting beneath the strings of a Stratocaster? Moreover, harps need to have strong strings because their strings are so long and pulled so tight. In any case, the mood of the song is mournful and elegiac, which fits the harp better than the guitar.

While some of King David's psalms bemoan the singer's plight and cry against the silence of God, others portray all of nature singing God's praises, and these are the ones closest in theology to Dylan's song. Let the whole earth make a joyful noise to God, sings the psalmist (Psalm 66). The Psalms, however, are always careful to imagine nature's noise as a response to God without identifying nature as a part of God, and Dylan follows this pattern. Nature echoes divine speech rather than speaking directly in God's voice. Evidence of this pattern is found in the way Dylan uses a simile, and not a metaphor, in the fourth stanza, where he describes the ocean being played *like* an organ. A pantheist would connect the ocean more directly to the organ (and give the organ its own agency), thereby metaphorically fusing (if not confusing) nature, humanity, and the divine, but the "like" keeps these elements apart. Indeed, there is a remarkable ambiguity about the voice in that stanza. If the ocean is "like an organ played," who is playing it? Is the ocean played in the sense of being played out, or is it playing with the seaweed? The ocean functions as something dangerous in the Psalms, and yet it can still be part of the universe's chorus of praise. Dylan again follows suit. He does not treat nature as the site for some kind of New Age eco-spirituality. The waves clash against the rocks and sands. There is turbulence here. Peace must be gained through suffering; heaven is promised to those whose journey involves carrying the cross.

Second, there is an obvious connection in this second stanza between the clashing cymbals and the rhetoric of the Apostle Paul. Paul compares faith without love to a "clanging cymbal" in 1 Corinthians 13:1. He probably associated the use of cymbals with paganism and preferred the simple singing of psalms over instrumental music in worship (see Colossians 3:16). Pagans went to worship to be transported into wordless states of ecstasy. As Paul reminds the converts he has made, "You know that when you were pagans, you were enticed and led astray to idols that could not speak" (1 Corinthians 12:2). The idols stood silent as musicians played aggressive and seductive sounds. What Paul is arguing against, in fact, is the very drug music that Gray finds expressed in Dylan's song. Dylan, however, is on Paul's side. Dylan is perpetuating Paul's suspicion of the use of loud noises to induce a counterfeit state of hypnotic spirituality with his turbulent image of waves crashing like cymbals clashing "against the rocks and sands."

Third, Dylan drew from the Hebrew Prophets, especially their wild expectations that God will renew or recreate the world. The sixth stanza is where this eschatological imagery comes fully into play. Eschatology is the study of the last things, and this song is clearly concerned with the world that is ending and the one that is yet to come. Dylan's vision of the singer standing "unwound" beneath "clouds unbound by laws" is a worthy heir of the way the Hebrew prophets imagined a day when God will redeem the world by creating it anew. Dylan's arresting image points to the liberation of nature, which, like humanity, is bound to the law of sin. Clouds, of course, are extremely unpredictable, blowing across the sky as if they follow no law, and yet even clouds are subjected to the laws of physics that determine all movement on Earth. That is what makes this phrase so striking in its eccentricity. Imagine, Dylan is saying, what clouds unbound by law will look like! Even the singer in Dylan's song is departing from this world's laws. This is the significance of "unwound," a delightful word that suggests he had been tightly wound before, but now he is as free as the clouds.

The Bible is actually full of cloud references, perhaps in order to dethrone the pagan association of the gods with the sky. Isaiah imagines God riding on a swift cloud (19:1), and Ezekiel says that the coming of the Lord "will be a day of clouds" (30:3). Several New Testament texts continue this motif by placing Christ's Second Coming in the clouds (Matthew 26:64 and Revelation 1:7). When John imagines the Son of Man seated on a cloud, he is picturing God as more powerful than the most unpredictable elements of nature (Revelation 14:14). That is, John is imagining clouds unbound by law.

After this demonstration of lyrical perfection in two tight lines about the unwound and the unbound, the sixth stanza takes a turn that comes close to something maudlin. The crying rain is a stock image, but Dylan ties it into a trumpet and then states that it "asked for no applause," so that the rhyming in the stanza is quietly moving. What is also powerful about the image is the odd juxtaposition of the sound of the rain and a trumpet. In an incredibly efficient manner, Dylan is hinting at how the sadness of the rain will sound as triumphant as a trumpet when the judgment day comes. Rather than evoking tears with its softness and its steady downpour, the rain will blare up and out, without asking for any response from us at all. The prophet Isaiah, in an equally surreal vision, writes about the coming day when the trees will clap their hands (55:12). Isaiah imagines the trees applauding God, while Dylan imagines nature being so dominated by God that no applause is necessary.

Fourth, and finally, there is the overwhelming presence of the Book of Revelation in this song. Dylan is a close reader of the Bible's climax, the Book of Revelation, and in no other song does he pay more loving tribute to that book. Revelation is sometimes taken as a vengeful text, but it follows in the tradition of the Hebrew prophets and their mystical visions. It contains not only startling visual images of the coming kingdom of God, but also sensitive auditory descriptions of the end times. Voices speak like thunder, and the singing is loud. Like Dylan, Revelation is trying to imagine a new world of sound. Twice in "Lay Down Your Weary Tune" Dylan speaks of the sound of a bugle or a trumpet, and in Revelation we read about John that "I was in the Spirit on the Lord's day, and I heard behind me a loud voice like a trumpet" (1:10). John is anticipating Dylan's song by imagining the voice of Jesus Christ as sufficiently powerful to take on a variety of acoustical forms.

Revelation has what I think is the most abrupt sonic shift, which results in the most stunning sonic image, in all of Western literature. After the Lamb of God opens the book with the seven seals, and after it is announced that God will wipe away all of the tears of those who believe, comes this verse: "When the Lamb opened the seventh seal, there was silence in heaven for about half an hour" (8:1). Imagine a pure silence that can be measured without anxiety and experienced with absolute peace and joy! Why does this silence last only half an hour? Perhaps because this is the first time that anyone has been able to hear what silence really sounds like. Perhaps silence of this magnitude would be so sublime that half an hour is all anyone could endure.

This moment echoes a story from the Old Testament about God's revelation to Elijah on Mount Horeb (1 Kings 19:9–18). In that story, God puts on a show for Elijah of a great wind, an earthquake, and a fire, but God's voice is not in any of these natural phenomena. Instead, after the fire, God speaks in the sound of sheer silence. These two passages are telling us what silence sounds like, since silence speaks only to those who have heard the sound of God. Silence for the spiritually deaf, therefore, is nothing. If there is no God, then silence is not even silent. That is, nothingness will engulf even silence in the end of time, and the contrast between sound and silence will be no more. Silence can be lonely and discordance noisy only if sound is ultimately harmonious and healing. Eastern meditation is a means of stilling silence by making peace with its emptiness, but the Bible teaches that silence is not nothing. The redemption of sound in heaven will make silence sing. This is a silence that is rich and full. This, in fact, is the silence that "no voice can hope to hum."

In a song about the end of all singing, Dylan cannot sing that which lies beyond the tune. So he has recourse to a passive image with "branches bare like a banjo played," hinting at the author and source of all sound. (In the Carnegie Hall concert version, Dylan sings "moaned" for "played," perhaps in order to avoid repeating the use of "played" in "an organ played" from the fourth stanza.) The image of the last leaves clinging to a new love's breast is definitely christological. It was standard usage in nineteenth century hymns to speak of faith as a matter of leaning on Jesus' breast. The source of this image is the Gospel of John: "Now there was leaning on Jesus' bosom one of his disciples, whom Jesus loved" (13:23, King James Version). Two verses later, this version of the Bible, which is the one Dylan prefers, uses the word *breast* when it identifies this disciple as the one "lying on Jesus' breast" (verse 25). This description has often troubled the great religious painters of Western history, who have had to surmount the compositional problem of putting the disciples around a table while having one of them lie, awkwardly, on Jesus' breast. Visually it is tricky, but the word "breast" has entered poetry and song as a synecdoche for Jesus. (A synecdoche uses a part as symbolic of a whole.) Gray thinks that the breast stands for nature, so that the leaves are entering the sacred earth, but the breast is too well known in the gospel hymns that influenced this song—hymns like "The Christian's Good Night"—for it to stand for anything other than Jesus Christ.

The final stanza before the return to the chorus plays on the baptismal image of a river. In Revelation 14, John hears "a voice from heaven like the sound of many waters" (verse 2). That same voice also sounds like "harpists playing on their harps" (verse 2). These two images—water and harps—ground this stanza. Later in Revelation, when John describes the New Jerusalem, central to its landscape is "the river of the water of life, bright as crystal," flowing through the middle of the city (22:1). In a brilliant leap of imagination, Dylan equates the strumming that he hears with the winding of the river. The water is so clear that it is like a mirror. One can almost imagine that Jesus himself is singing, because the singer sees in the mirror of the river the hymn that nobody else can hum. In any case, Dylan evokes multiple meanings with this river. Christians find salvation in the water of baptism, and Dylan's singer finds the hymn he wants to hear in the running of the water. Dylan mixes the visual and the auditory to create a consummate image bursting with the joy of anticipation amidst the sorrow of letting go. It is as if sound has saturated everything, so that every physical movement carries sonic weight. This makes sense, of course, because sound is borne aloft by vibrations in the air. Lest we be led astray, however, it is crucial to remember that nature is not speaking on its own behalf. It is the hum that animates the world, bringing all things to life. The hum at the end of the world is God.

God's voice can melt the earth, the psalmist tells us (Psalm 46:6). Another psalm anticipates the half hour of heavenly silence in Revelation 8:1: "He made the storm be still, and the waves of the sea were hushed. Then they were glad because they had quiet, and he brought them to their desired haven" (Psalm 107:29–30). Between these two audio poles—God's unimaginable voice and a silence redeemed by sound—lies Dylan's song. Each of us has, or is, a weary tune. To enter into grace is to realize that while we think we are playing, we are actually being played. God is strumming our hearts. We think that if we rest for a moment, a destructive silence will descend. When we lay down our tune for the last time, however, we will come to hear how our song is but a part of the whole. Jesus is the strength of strings who gives us rest.

How Dylan wrote this song no one knows. It must have been a singular gift of grace that lifted this tune from the noisy din of rock and roll. "Lay Down Your Weary Tune" is the most honest and heartfelt salute to what the world is on the basis of what it will yet become, if we but pass through it like pilgrims to a better place. If you were to be given the grace of being conscious at the moment of your death, to hear this song as you depart this world would be an act of the supererogatory sublime. This is a lullaby to the end of time, God's goodnight kiss to us in the form of a song. It is, in fact, one of the greatest theological songs since King David composed his psalms.

Notes

1. Bob Dylan, *Chronicles, Volume One*, p. 90.

2. The quote is from Marjorie Guthrie's daughter, Nora, in Sounes, *Down the Highway*, p. 83.

3. For a fascinating survey of how people spoke and heard before the twentieth century, see Richard Cullen Roth, *How Early America Sounded* (Ithaca: Cornell University Press, 2003).

4. Paul Friedlander, *Rock and Roll: A Social History* (Boulder: Westview Press, 1996), p. 88.

5. *Biograph*, p. 24.

6. John Updike, *Concerts at Castle Hill, H. H., John Updike's Middle Initial Reviews Local Music in Ipswich, Massachusetts, from 1961 to 1965* (Northridge: Lord John Press, 1993), pp. 39–40.

7. *Younger Than That Now*, p. 146.

8. Sounes, *Down the Highway*, p. 67.

9. From the comment by Arthur Rosato in Heylin, *Behind the Shades Revisited*, p. 364.

10. Alec Wilkinson, "The Protest Singer: Pete Seeger and American Folk Music," *The New Yorker*, April 17, 2006, p. 47.

11. See Terry Alexander Gans, *What's Real and What Is Not, Bob Dylan Through 1964: The Myth of Protest* (Munich, West Germany: Hobo Press, 1983), p. 39. Published nearly fourteen years after it was written, this was the first book to seriously challenge the image of Dylan as a political protest singer.

12. I draw this insight from Sounes, *Down the Highway*, p. 21.

13. G. W. F. Hegel, *First Philosophy of Spirit (Part III of the System of Speculative Philosophy, 1803/4)*, ed. and trans. H. S. Harris and T. M. Knox (Albany: Statue University of New York Press, 1979), p. 222.

14. Scobie, *Alias Bob Dylan Revisited*, p. 66.

15. Scaduto, *Bob Dylan*, pp. 259–60.

16. Baez, *And a Voice to Sing With*, p. 91.

17. Ibid., p. 95.

18. Greil Marcus, *Invisible Republic: Bob Dylan's Basement Tapes* (New York: Henry Holt, 1977), p. 87.

19. Recent scholarship has demonstrated how advances in technology changed not only the way we listen to music but also the way performers play music. Sound has become so easily manipulated that music has become dematerialized and desocialized, to the point where listening is a private experience and the difference between an artist and an engineer begins to disappear. Much popular singing today sounds disembodied because of the artificial clarity that technology brings to the recording process. Records, rather than preserving live performances, have become works of art. Transparent reproduction was once the goal of recording technology, but now music does not sound right unless it is manipulated and transformed by various production techniques. Dylan sings in spite of the fact that he is being recorded, rather than for the recording. You can hear his body in his voice, from his head to his toes. For further analysis of how technology has changed the way music is played and heard, see Robert Philip, *Performing Music in the Age of Recording* (New Haven: Yale University Press, 2004); and Mark Katz, *Capturing Sound: How Technology Has Changed Music* (Berkeley: University of California Press, 2004). For the most perceptive and engaging examination of the way digital music is stretching sound in disembodies shapes, see David Toop, *Haunted Weather: Music, Silence and Memory* (London: Serpent's Tail, 2004). Toop describes electronic musical experiments that use improvisation, randomness, noise, environment, and even blindfolds in order to take sound to its most dehumanized limit.

20. Some commentators speculate that the song was directed at Joan Baez (as a way of urging her to move beyond her folk repertoire), but this seems unlikely, given that Dylan never took Baez that seriously. Dylan wrote it right before her October 17 concert at the Hollywood Bowl, and evidently, Dylan asked her to perform it with him. The song was barely finished at that point and Baez did not know all the words, so they stumbled through it. See the account of this period in David Hajdu, *Positively 4th Street: The Lives and Times of Joan Baez, Bob Dylan, Mimi Baez Farina, and Richard Farina* (New York: North Point Press, 2001), pp. 189–90.

21. Christopher Ricks, *Dylan's Vision of Sin* (New York: Harper-Collins, 2003), p. 132.

22. Gray, *Song and Dance Man III*, p. 197.

23. John Herdman has also made this claim in *Voice Without Restraint: A Study of Bob Dylan's Lyrics and Their Background* (New York: Deliah Books, 1981), p. 92.

24. Gray, *Song and Dance Man III*, p. 204.

25. Ibid., p. 197.

26. Ibid.

27. "The drugs at the end of the '60s were artificial. . . . I was never involved in the acid scene either." Interview with Lynne Allen, *Trouser Press*, Dec. 12, 1976, reprinted in *Younger Than That Now*, p. 167.

CHAPTER FIVE

A Tale of
Two Popes

At the end of September 1997, Bob Dylan found himself playing before the Pope. The occasion was the World Eucharist Congress in Bologna, Italy. Over one hundred thousand were in attendance, with millions more Europeans watching the concert on a live TV broadcast. Dylan sang, appropriately, "Knockin' on Heaven's Door" for John Paul II, who appeared at one point to be snoozing during the show. At the end of his set, Dylan took off his Stetson and climbed the dais to greet the religious leader of one-fifth of the world's population. John Paul II, for his part, appropriated Dylan's most famous lyrics for his sermon. "You say that answer is blowing in the wind, my friend. So it is: But it is not the wind that blows things away. It is the wind that is the breath and life of the Holy Spirit, the voice that calls and says, 'Come!'" John Paul was showing that he could be a performer too.

John Paul II might have been upstaging Dylan, but he was not misinterpreting "Blowin' in the Wind." Anyone who was as immersed in the Bible and midwestern culture as Dylan could not have written that song without thinking, consciously or unconsciously, about the connection made in the Bible between the Spirit and the wind. I grew up singing that song every year at church camp, usually at night while we gathered around a bonfire. The fire made it seem as if we were conjuring the sound of the wind with our singing. At the time, I didn't know who had written "Blowin' in the Wind," but I was under the impression that it was an old Christian hymn! That song still reminds me of one particular saying of Jesus, "The wind blows where it chooses, and you hear the sound of it, but you do not know where it comes from or where it is goes. So it is with everyone who is born of the Spirit" (John 3:8). This connection is more than metaphor. Hebrew *ruach* and Greek *pneuma* can both mean breath, air, wind, spirit, or soul.

That Dylan and the Pope got together should have been no surprise. John Paul II was often called the rock 'n' roll Pope. Young people were attracted to his charisma in droves. He called for the first World Youth Day celebration in Rome in 1985, and these events quickly became some of the largest gatherings in the world. When he died, the media paid him tribute by observing that he had the aura of a rock star. This was said so many times that nobody stopped to think how odd a comparison it was. The magnitude of the fame of rock stars is undeserved and fleeting. It derives from a distortion of the power saints once had to hold people up to the highest moral standards. Stars burn out so quickly because they shine with the borrowed light of our own envious desires, while saints burn with an enduring passion for the good.

The fame of rock stars also derives from the Protestant revivalism of the nineteenth century and the black worship styles shaped by African traditions of spirit possession. As Teresa

L. Reed observes, in a perceptive analysis of the influence of black gospel music on rock and roll, "Black worshippers commonly allow sacred music to fill them with such inspiration that physical expression becomes a natural response. Dancing, screaming, and fainting are not at all unusual in these settings."[1] White America had its own traditions of emotionally expressive worship styles, but old-fashioned revivals had become marginalized by the middle of the twentieth century. For the average Anglo-American growing up after World War II, collective displays of exuberance were connected to rock, not religion. Such behavior had to be learned from concerts performed by singers like Sam Cooke, who had crossed over from careers in the black churches into popular music.

Unsurprisingly, rock stars are often ruined by their fame. Charismatic preachers too can abuse their power, but Pentecostal churches, at their best, sublimate physical passion into an ecstatic experience that transcends the moral realm without transgressing particular moral rules. Rock-and-roll concerts can descend into public and private acts of destruction because they leave the passions they stir with no positive moral direction. The stimulation of rock, in other words, serves no constructive purpose. Drugs and sex are inevitable components of the rock world because it is so empty. Rock stars become trapped by their fans in prisons of projected desire. In an attempt to break out of these scripted performances of excessive behavior, many of them dabble in left-wing political posturing, but the use of radical politics to rationalize their inordinate influence over young people is too transparent to be taken seriously. Rock singers who try to change the world often end up becoming false prophets.

For all these reasons and more, comparing John Paul II to a rock star is like declaring that an original painting is a good likeness to its counterfeit. Far from trying to rock the world, the Pope was just being holy—but he was also showing the world that the Catholic Church still represents the origin as well as the universal pinnacle of all holiness. His charisma was just a way of bringing it all back home.

With the election of Joseph Cardinal Ratzinger to the papacy, many suspected that the party was over. In contrast to their treatment of John Paul II, the media often portray Benedict XVI striking a dour pose. John Paul II was a Polish philosopher eager to lead the church into a new era. Benedict XVI, a German theologian, is pessimistic about the possibility that social activism can usher in the kingdom of God. Benedict XVI served as a theological consultant at the Second Vatican Council (1962–65), which modernized Catholic doctrine and practice, but he has since had second thoughts. He has spent much of his subsequent scholarly career trying to keep the liberal interpretations of that Council in check.[2]

The portrait of Benedict XVI as a bulldog defending every iota of traditional church dogma is a caricature at best. He is, in fact, one of the most sophisticated theologians of our time. He has also written some of the most perceptive and provocative analyses of music in general, and rock and roll in particular, of any religious leader in the past generation. All of Pope Benedict XVI's reflections on music take their cue from the liturgy of the Mass. This is not because of a compulsive attachment to tradition for its own sake. Rather, Benedict XVI is convinced that our proper existence in the world must be grounded in our relationship to God, and he is further convinced that our relationship to God is most essentially expressed in worship. The goal of worship is to prepare us for a life of freedom and love.

Benedict XVI is sensitive to the role of sound in Christian worship. The Second Vatican Council encouraged the congregation's participation in the Mass by making the priest celebrant more involved with the laity and permitting the substitution of vernacular languages for Latin. As the prefect of the Congregation for the Doctrine of the Faith, a post he held until his election to the papacy, Ratzinger insisted that these changes did not comprise a call for liturgical revolution. In fact, he warned against any innovations that might open the door to commotion and noise. Nothing should distract from the prayerful silence that is the foundation of Christian worship.

Silence, however, is not an end in itself. The church is the place where Christians listen to the Word of God. Ratzinger applauded the Second Vatican Council's efforts to put more emphasis on scripture and proclamation in the liturgy. Even at its stillest point, worship is comprised of linguistic acts of communication. Nevertheless, when the mystery of God is involved, words are not enough. This is why Benedict XVI, when he writes about the liturgy, gives close attention to church architecture and other material and non-spoken aspects of worship.

Where the liturgy most dramatically moves beyond spoken words is in song. This movement beyond speaking endows music with its nearly sacred significance. Singing, for Benedict XVI, is a gift of the Holy Spirit, with roots that go back to the Old Testament. Singing makes its first appearance in the Bible after the Israelites have crossed the Red Sea (Exodus 15:1). For the Jews, songs born of praise reach their biblical climax with the psalms of David. Christians hear in these psalms a cry for Jesus. Christ is the true liberation from all forms of bondage, which makes it most appropriate to respond to his sacrifice in song. Songs of praise have the peculiar characteristic of what Benedict XVI calls a "sober inebriation."[3] Spirituality disconnected from the moral goodness of God can lead in any direction, and certainly the spirit of music can easily result in various kinds of harmful intoxication.

That is why it is important to realize that the Holy Spirit is not just any kind of spirit. The Holy Spirit does not stand alone, just as it never stands still. It is the gift of Jesus Christ as well as of God the Father. The Spirit blows where it will, but its manifestations are determined by the identity of God. The identity of God is, of course, made known in Jesus Christ, and one of the chief titles of Christ is the Logos, taken from the prologue to the Gospel of John. *Logos* is a Greek term that means word, reason, or plan. While music can conjure many kinds of spirit, praise that is filled by the Holy Spirit is a gift that does not distract from reason, which has its source in the Word of God.

As a rule, then, instrumental music should never drown out the words of a sung text. Benedict XVI notes that some early Christians were tempted by inroads of Eastern mysticism to dissolve the good news into an emotional fusion of poetry and music. The church understandably reacted by restricting the use of instrumental music in worship. The fifty-ninth canon of the Council of Laodicea (364) forbade the use of privately composed hymns in the Mass. Singing was restricted to psalms sung by the choir. This represented a return to the purely vocal style of singing inherited from the Jewish synagogue. Benedict XVI applauds the opening of worship to musical instruments in the Middle Ages, but he warns against the potential dangers of instruments dominating the human voice. History shows us how the church has had to step in to correct musical excesses. When church music became more sophisticated in the late Middle Ages, musicians began claiming the right of artistic freedom. Secular music was no longer born of reverence and prayer. Sacred and secular musicians began competing with each other. The Council of Trent had to intervene to limit once again the use of instruments in worship.

The Catholic Church is not biased against instrumental music. On the contrary, much of the best instrumental music in Western history has been inspired by the Mass and has tried to pay wordless tribute to the majesty of Christian worship. The Catholic Church has long admitted that even in the most secular music, especially of the classical variety, listeners can hear God being glorified. Despite Catholicism's efforts to hold together secular and sacred music, however, the gap between them has widened in the modern world into a nearly unbridgeable chasm.

At its best, the laws of music comprise a harmonious structure that acts like the order of creation to organize human freedom and limit its excesses. Musicians must submit to the mathematical structure of music just as scientists must submit to the laws of nature and, in submission, the world can be properly enjoyed, while creativity becomes an act of joy. The more music becomes an outlet for idiosyncratic and experimental personal passions, Benedict XVI laments, the less it reflects its divine source. When music is invested with idolatrous passion, there is "the threat of the virtuoso mentality, the vanity of technique, which is no longer the servant of the whole but wants to push itself to the fore."[4] Even the church can become a victim of musical passion when operatic elements enter the Mass.

Benedict XVI's objective is not to turn the clock back on musical history. He does not want to standardize all music according to church dogma. Nonetheless, his argument is ambitious. In its pronouncements about music, the Catholic Church has kept its focus on the conduct of worship, but it has also insisted that the practice of worship has implications that reach beyond Sunday morning. Benedict XVI follows this tradition. He concedes that classical music has become something of an "elitist ghetto," but that is why musicians still need the church. The church, he insists, should be the source of nothing less than a universal culture. All art should be measured by its ultimate service to the Word of God. This does not mean that all music must be church music. On the contrary, the church should be the wellspring for all music, but not all music needs to be playable on Sunday mornings. For music to have meaning, Benedict XVI seems to be saying, it must be measured by something it is not. It also must have some kind of unity. Otherwise, music will be nothing more than an accompaniment to our subjective emotional states.

What this means in practical terms is that heavenly music must be grounded in human speech. Music need not always be commentary on a sacred text, but that is the form to which it should strive. The liturgy, after all, centers on the proclamation of the cross of Christ in the Word and in the Eucharist. In an arresting phrase, Benedict XVI says that "faith becoming music is part of the process of the Word becoming flesh."[5] In this incarnational way, music elevates earthly material like brass, strings, and human flesh to new emotional heights. Composers can find the elements of song in all aspects of creation because the world was made to be the stage for the incarnation. Music accompanies that drama, but it should not overwhelm it by upstaging human speech with sounds that are destructive to the act of communication. Singing, Benedict XVI concludes, should always have priority in the liturgy over instrumental music. The Mass is structured according to a dialogue. The call from God is mediated by the priest, and the congregation responds. Music finds its role as a response to God's initiative of grace. Like silence, music is made holy by the preaching of the Word and the reading of scripture. It is not an end in itself.

The music of the church should be an inspiration for all musicians. Church music is nothing less than cosmic in scope, because we praise God alongside all of creation. When this cosmic scope is forgotten or neglected, music turns into a mere expression of the composer's will. It might dramatize a personal struggle, but it says little about the destiny of the world—and even less about God. Nevertheless, Benedict XVI admits that the church is not currently in a position to provide a universal culture for the development of authentically beautiful music. We live in a period of history when popular culture is in need of purification, rather than encouragement and accommodation. There is much talk of culture wars, but there is also a sound war raging all around us. The church needs to practice its music today in opposition to the music of the world.

Music should purify the senses rather than gratify them with the false promise of an ecstatic and frenzied release from the toils of the everyday. This promise is false because people can never find fulfillment in the deliberate destruction of their personal integrity. That is the problem with much rock and roll. Listening to rock on the radio is like listening to someone flaunting his or her private obsessions. Likewise, going to a rock concert is like watching thousands of people flaunting their private obsessions all in one place. Benedict XVI is very sensitive to the power of music to form communal bonds. When music is reduced to individual creativity, it forms a community that is of and for the moment, without regard for anything greater than itself. For Benedict XVI, rock concerts have a cultic character that puts them in direct opposition to Christian worship. Rock, he says, is industrially produced and aimed at the masses. There is nothing sober or lasting about the resulting inebriation. "In ecstasy of having all their defenses torn down, the participants sink, as it were, beneath the elemental force of the universe."[6] An essential part of the ideology of rock is that individuals can only express themselves outside of social institutions. Rock preaches over and over again the idea that institutions suppress individual freedom. Correspondingly, the liturgy of rock is of a do-it-yourself variety that cannot point to anything greater than the whimsies of the narcissistic self.

Word of Benedict XVI's criticisms of rock and roll have gotten out on the Internet, and though I have not seen any scholarly discussions of his remarks, he is already being disparaged on blogs and Web sites as a curmudgeonly killjoy who just does not get it. What he says, however, sounds a lot like some things Bob Dylan has said about the rock world. In an interview with Cameron Crowe that was included in *Biograph*, Dylan complains about what rock and roll has become. The context is some reminiscing about the excitement that surrounded his decision to reunite with The Band in 1974. They recorded *Planet Waves* and then announced Dylan's first coast-to-coast tour, which sold out in hours. They recreated their controversial shows of 1965–66, but this time, as Dylan points out, the fans were ready. In 1965, Dylan sounded like nothing anybody had ever heard. In 1975, the fans expected him to sound just the same as he had then. As Dylan explained to Crowe, "The people that came out to see us came mostly to see what they missed the first time around." For Dylan and The Band, it was mindless and emotionless playing. They were reproducing what they had done before. The fans were too busy consuming the aura of a legend to listen too carefully to the sound.

Dylan had created one of the most commercially and critically acclaimed rock tours in history, yet he knew he could never perform that way again. Rock and roll had become a spectacle, and Dylan is a storyteller. Concerts were circus shows with debilitating noise and freaky lighting. "That's what it had become and that's what it still is," Dylan told Crowe. "It is like those guys who watched the H bomb explode on Bikini Island and then turn to each other and say, 'Beautiful, man, just incredibly beautiful.'" Dylan is pointing out the difference between Christian and pagan versions of the end of the world. In Christian apocalypse, the coming end is associated with moral judgment and the transformation of the world into a just and righteous kingdom. In pagan apocalypse, the end is just the end. Rock concerts are clearly closer to the pagan variety of total destruction than the Christian version of transformation. Pagan theology can be summarized by the old saying that is known by the biblical writers: Eat, drink and be merry, for tomorrow we will die (Isaiah 22:13 and Ecclesiastes 8:15).

In the same interview, Dylan continues with the military comparison: "Actually it was just big industry moving in on the music. Like the armaments manufacturers selling weapons to both sides in a war, inventing bigger and better things to take your head off while behind your back, there's a few people laughing and getting rich off your vanity."[7] These were more than just throwaway comments. Dylan was testifying to the way rock concerts had become pagan rituals dramatizing both self-indulgence and self-destruction. Indeed, self-indulgence is the quickest way to self-destruction, and rock provided the directions.

Dylan could be accused of nostalgia. He came of age when a singer could walk into a studio with a guitar and a couple of friends and make a great record. He never liked the recording process very much, although he liked being in control. By the seventies, the technology of rock had passed him by. By the eighties, his grand days of filling stadiums with the sheer power of his will were also over. Perhaps he was nostalgic for the days when he played in coffeehouses, but perhaps he had also gained some wisdom and perspective along the way. In any case, he and the new Pope had come to very similar conclusions about the pagan nature of most rock concerts. Dylan had been the object of zealous worship, and the experience was never gratifying. Though he made millions from his fame, he understood the pathology behind his riches. He was not a saint; he was not even a good moral example. He was either a victim or a beneficiary, depending on how you look at it, of very dark times.

Dylan illuminated his times, but he could also hide in the darkness. His artistic triumph, as well as his various personal tragedies and his eventual ability to come to terms with himself through religion, can be understood only if they are put in the right context. The utopian clamor of the sixties sounds to us today like a parody of a religious revival, with radicals preaching the overthrow of the "system" and hippies trying to get back to the garden of Eden. That decade was so religiously confused that music became the only answer many young people could trust. Many factors contributed to the growing spiritual restlessness of America in the sixties, but the most relevant for the history of rock music is the changing nature of higher education.

Beginning in the late fifties, universities began abandoning the *in loco parentis* system that had restricted student behavior on co-ed campuses.[8] Before this time, colleges and universities were expected to reinforce social and parental authority over students. As enrollments at universities surged, this became increasingly problematic for practical reasons. The personal and unquestioned authority of deans of students gave way to impersonal rules that soon broke down over challenges about student rights. Rules were clarified, but even perfect procedures do not produce community. Students were increasingly entrusted with all of the privileges of adulthood and few of the responsibilities of citizenship.

The new emphasis on student freedom was not just a practical response to burgeoning enrollments and the number of older students returning from military service. More fundamentally, authority over sexual behavior began shifting out of the hands of social custom and into the hands of experts. Government agencies were becoming more important than churches in setting the mood for sexual morality. The unsettling of local cultures that began with the mobilization of millions of young men for World War II continued with the growing economy and the rise of state schools to national popularity. Students began going away for college, rather than staying close to home. In order to broaden their enrollment base, colleges that were founded by Christian churches began turning their backs on their religious traditions. With no moral foundation to enforce, college personnel were forced into a moral relativism in order to support and nurture the student body. Student health clinics replaced chaplaincies as the place to go for sexual advice. Curfews were out; coed dorms were in. Youth had become its own culture, and anxiety over sexual freedom was in need of assuagement. The environment was ripe for the triumph of rock and roll.

When Dylan first found his voice, he appealed to young people who were alienated from conventional music and religion alike. Most of Dylan's contemporaries had had some kind of religious upbringing, but they often did not know anything about the substance of their faith. Their parents raised them with a strict morality stripped of any theological depth. Dylan, for example, had been bar mitzvahed as a teenager, in 1954, by an Orthodox rabbi from Brooklyn who showed up just in time for his religious instruction and left soon afterward. The rabbi was too orthodox for the assimilated Jews of Hibbing, Minnesota. Dylan's father, like most fathers at that time, was morally strict. When he accepted his Lifetime Achievement Award at the Grammy ceremony in 1991, Dylan opened up about his father. "My daddy once said to me, he said, 'Son, it is possible for you to become so defiled in this world that your own Mother and Father will abandon you. If that happens, God will believe in your own ability to mend your own ways.'" Contrary to some of the stories Dylan liked to tell about himself in his early years, he was raised with solid midwestern values.

What set Dylan apart from many of his peers was his knowledge of the Bible, which, given the precipitous decline in biblical literacy after World War II, was notable for its depth and proficiency. Dylan's immersion in the Bible can be explained by his musical preferences. Much of the music he was drawn to was steeped in biblical themes and theological motifs. When Dylan found a way to reinvigorate that music, he became nearly godlike to fans looking for new heroes to take the place of dying traditions. He made it clear from the beginning of his career, with the song "Hero Blues," that he never wanted to play that game. His rejection of the celebrity trap had a spiritual basis, since he was searching for truth beyond anything what could be made by human hands alone. He was probably led in this direction by his own songwriting, since he always talks about it as a gift from beyond his own efforts. His best lyrics come to him like undeserved grace.

As much as Dylan has tried to deflect attention away from his personal life, many fans continue to ponder his inner mental states, as if his psyche is the golden gateway into the mysteries of his music. Pope Benedict XVI is right to be suspicious of the dismal dynamics of stardom. Music that does not lead to God inevitably leads to idolatry. The latest form of Dylanolatry is the ongoing scrutiny given to the state of Dylan's soul. Anytime I mention to someone that I am writing this book, he or she asks me if Dylan is still a Christian or tells me that he is not. Some have claimed to know that he has returned to Judaism, while others insist that his evangelical period was just a passing fad.

Backsliding is an ordinary aspect of the Christian life, but has Dylan backed out of Christianity altogether? Those who were most critical of Dylan's conversion betray their own search for certainty by wanting a black or white answer to this question. They are bound to be disappointed if they expect Dylan to tell us what he believes. As Dylan himself has said, "I find the religiosity and philosophy in the music. . . . I believe the songs."[9] Dylan's theology is musical, and I will show later that not only has his music remained theological but he also has deepened his understanding of the relationship between faith and doubt.

Beyond tabloid gossip about Dylan's private life, his celebrity coupled with his conversion does raise some fundamental questions about the role of religion in modern American society. In particular, Dylan's biography, at least what we know of it, raises the troubling problem of whether one can be a musical saint without being a moral role model. There are numerous examples of geniuses who have been wantonly immoral, but what about a genius who wants to be a Christian? Does being a musical genius exempt you from being a moral person? Dylan himself has answered that question in the negative. "You can be a priest and be in rock 'n' roll. Being a rock 'n' roll singer is no different from being a house painter."[10] Nevertheless, as Pope Benedict XVI has argued, there is something about rock and roll that cuts against the grain of Christian morality.

Those of us who are not stars can be sympathetic to Dylan's plight without excusing him. The New Testament does not say much about fame, but it does talk about fortune. Jesus lectured on the difficulties a rich man faces in trying to enter the kingdom of God. Celebrities compound the spiritual burden of wealth with the unreality of fame. As one of the world's most mysterious and sought-after celebrities, Bob Dylan cannot live a normal lifestyle nor have an ordinary existence. So Christians cannot expect Dylan to be a traditional, churchgoing, everyday witness to the faith. Or can they? It is hard to imagine Dylan attending a local church without causing a disturbance. Christians at worship would not hound him, but their gawking would probably distract him (and others) from communion with God. I have a hard time imagining Dylan singing traditional hymns in the pew behind me. For one thing, his voice would be too distinct to blend easily into the sound of the congregation. For another, the worshippers around him would probably lower their voices in order to hear his! Whatever we might think about the troubles that follow upon fame, Dylan must keep as much of his life private as he can for reasons having to do with both his security and his art—let alone his sanity. This surely makes being a member of the visible body of Christ difficult.

Dylan's spiritual development also raises the interesting question of the relationship between Judaism and Christianity. If Dylan is self-conscious about going to church, imagine the hard choices he is faced with concerning any participation in Jewish activities. There are those in the media who track his every visit to Israel and document any donations he gives to Jewish causes. If the media were really interested in his spiritual exploration of Judaism, that would be fine, but the obsessive nature of this attention suggests that there is a lot of discomfort when a famous Jew converts to Christianity. Those keeping tabs on his trips to Israel are not just reporting; they are keeping score, and hoping that Judaism wins. It would be easier that way, since a Jew who returns to Judaism is more acceptable than a Jew who finds Jesus.

As early as 1984, Dylan was so tired of being hounded about his religious views that he denied he was "born again." That's just another label people use, he said, to dismiss views they don't want to bother thinking about. And he was right: "born again" was shorthand for "religious zealot." At the time, Dylan was moving beyond the particular brand of evangelicalism that he converted to, but he did not become a member of any specific denomination, as far as I know. He seemed to be exploring the theological implications of monotheism without, however, giving up on the centrality of Christ. "What it comes down to is that there's a lot of different gods in the world against the God—that's what it's about."[11] Dylan's spirituality is rooted in the monotheism of the prophets, and he sees Jesus as reinforcing that tradition. "What Jesus does for an ignorant man like myself is to make the qualities and characteristics of God more believable to me, 'cause I can't beat the devil. Only God can. He already has."[12] Christianity emerged at a time when Jews were under the rule of Rome, and Jews and Christians alike were struck by the pervasiveness of evil and the need for reliance on God's grace. Christianity ran with the twin themes of evil and grace, while Judaism developed an elaborate and loving relationship with ritual and the law. Dylan has always had a strong sense of sin and of the futility of human endeavor, which puts him on the Christian side of the Jewish-Christian divide.

In one of his longest discussions of the relationship between Judaism and Christianity from a 1981 interview, he said, "There's really no difference between any of it in my mind. Some people say they're Jews and they never go to the synagogue or anything. I know some gangsters who say they're Jews. I don't know what that's got to do with anything. Judaism is really the laws of Moses. If you follow the laws of Moses you're automatically a Jew I would think."[13] There is little evidence that Dylan has ever had a great desire to follow the laws of Moses. In an interview before his conversion to Christianity, Dylan explains that he did not think of himself as Jewish when he was growing up. "I've never felt Jewish. I really don't consider myself Jewish or non-Jewish. I don't have much of a Jewish background."[14] This has not stopped Wilfrid Mellers, among others, from trying to find some Jewish influence on Dylan's music. Mellers suggests that "the nasally inflected, melismatic style of cantilation found in extreme form in 'One More Cup of Coffee' is more pervasive than might at first be suspected."[15] After this observation, he goes on in a less speculative vein to demonstrate how Dylan's vocal landscape is thoroughly and expansively American, with particular connection to the mythology of the Wild West. Jews have contributed to the American experience, of course, but the sound of American music has been predominantly shaped by Christianity. Whether we like it or not, Dylan, like many Jewish converts to Christianity, was able to discover the riches of his ancestral heritage only after he experienced Christ as the Messiah the Jews had been expecting.

To what extent Dylan embraces his Jewish roots today is a matter of speculation, because he has stopped answering questions about his faith. (There are exceptions. In 1995, he was asked, "When you look ahead now, do you still see a Slow Train Coming?" He replied, "When I look ahead now, it's picked up quite a bit of speed. In fact, it's going like a freight train now."[16]) He is not running for Pope, he has said. Nobody asks Billy Joel what he believes in. The fact of the matter is that our society has little understanding of or tolerance for the ways in which Christianity and Judaism intimately intermingle in complex spiritual ways. Too many Christians, perhaps out of guilt about the Holocaust, treat Judaism as a museum artifact that needs careful preserving. Fundamentalist Christians still tend to treat the Hebraic covenant as broken and superseded by the church. Jewish leaders are understandably worried about intermarriage and the decline in the number of devout Jews. Only recently have Jewish intellectuals felt secure enough in their own religious status to begin the process of exploring the extent to which Judaism is as influenced by Christianity as Christianity is rooted in Judaism.[17]

Dylan's so-called return to Judaism, then, makes sense as a completion of his quest for the Messiah. Dylan inhabits that most challenging of categories, a Christian Jew or a Jewish Christian, which frustrates in equal portions people of strong faith and people with none.[18] In the aftermath of the Holocaust, a Jew who comes to believe that Jesus Christ fulfills the covenant God made with Israel is vulnerable to criticism on all sides. Some Christians suspect that messianic Jews have not fully converted to the true faith, while Jews cry betrayal. Secularists insist on eliminating the hyphen that has combined Judaism and Christianity as the twin foundations of Western culture. Our Judeo-Christian heritage is in shambles, with new gods proliferating at a dizzying rate. Dylan's truest expression of his Jewish heritage is his insistence that the countless gods we worship are manifestations of a pagan spirit.

Whether from necessity or choice, Dylan's public life is his music, and that is where we are forced to find his faith as well. His music is God's gift to him and his gift to us, and it is where he focuses all of his creative energy—and, we may presume, much of his spiritual energy as well. Critics tend to portray his musical development after *Slow Train Coming* as one happy return to the secular realm. It is as if he tried to rise too high and needed to regain his bearings by getting his feet firmly planted on the ground. This is a convenient narrative, because it allows his critics to tread lightly and quickly over his Christian period. It is also a wrongheaded narrative, since Dylan has always lived by the rule of "don't look back." He never repeats himself musically, so the fact that he has not continued recording in the gospel tradition is hardly evidence that he has tossed off his religious beliefs. As he told Robert Hilburn of the *L.A. Times*, "I've made my statement, and I don't think I could make it any better than in some of those songs. Once I've said what I need to say in a song, that's it. I don't want to repeat myself."[19] In fact, he turned his faith into a musical statement better than any white person alive. It would be impossible for him to recapture that accomplishment through repetition, even if he wanted to.

It is too simple to see Dylan's spiritual development as one of a fall into and then an escape from Christianity. I want to offer an alternative narrative. From the evidence of his music alone, it is clear that Dylan has continued to wrestle with his faith since *Slow Train Coming*, though his spiritual development is hardly linear in either an upward or a downward direction. Like most of us, he has matured, but he also has taken steps backward when he has wanted to go forward. The concept of progress belongs to the secular realm of technology rather than to the realm of the spirit. Biblical Christianity contains multiple narratives of the spiritual life, any one of which is not necessarily better than any other. The various patterns of spirituality to be found in the Bible function as grids onto which we can project our own lives. Dylan's gospel albums were exercises in revival, and revivals, by definition, are hard to sustain. Some people only hear the doom in revivals and draw the conclusion that evangelicalism is all about judgment and the end of the world. If that were the substance of the evangelical style of worship, it would hardly be so popular. Judgment and doom are preached as a call to change and action. The thought of the coming end of all things is enough to make believers clear their heads of popular culture and focus on purity of heart.

As important as revivalism is to American culture, including to the origins of rock and roll, there is an older spirituality that precedes it and, arguably, provides the surest foundation for a common understanding of American identity. Although America was religiously pluralistic from the very beginning of the European migration, one group stood out from the rest: the Puritans, who brought with them the theology of John Calvin, the great Protestant Reformer. Calvin's majestic theme was the sovereignty of God, which implies a strong doctrine of predestination. Few doctrines have been more grievously misunderstood. The doctrine of predestination is often taken to be a Christian variation of fatalism, but nothing could be further from the truth. The Puritans were hard workers, confident in their settlement of the New World and bold in their defense of the faith. Predestination does not result in spiritual immobility any more than the preaching of hellfire and damnation does. Predestination is a technical theological term that serves as the intellectual basis for the Christian's confidence in divine Providence. The Puritans debated the nuances of predestination, but they never doubted that God was in control of history.

Trust in Providence does not necessarily contradict the revivalist mentality that spread along America's vast western frontier in the eighteenth and nineteenth centuries. Revivalism and providentialism are two types of biblical spirituality that can and do coexist. Nonetheless, there are significant differences between their spiritual trajectories. Revivalism puts the emphasis on individual decision making, while Providence takes a long view of history and, from that long view, Providence puts human willing and doing in a diminished perspective.

The problem with revivalism is that it depends too much on human initiative and will power. It is, bluntly put, hard to keep up all the excitement. Far from drifting from his faith, Dylan can be seen as moving from a revivalist to a providential type of faith. His second Christian album, *Saved* (1980), is already evidence of this transformation. *Saved* is tight with tension. Dylan is shouting a bit too loudly about his faith on this album; consequently, he appears somewhat uncertain about his certainty. The album is frenetic with struggle rather than revival. Willfrid Mellers has perceptively observed about this album that "There is an element of frenzy, of course, in all gospel music, black or white, but this music, coming from a man who may be saved but is not and never was innocent in the sense that poor white and alienated black might be, has a slightly extravagant vehemence, as well as an uneasy edge."[20] Dylan is protesting against those who protest against his faith when he sings, on "Solid Rock," "And I can't let go, won't let go, and I can't let go no more." But in "What Can I Do For You," Dylan shows that he is moving beyond the more emotional aspects of revivalism by asking what he can give back to God. This album is also transitional in that it contains the first evidence of Dylan's renewed interest in Judaism. A passage from Jeremiah 31:3 is displayed prominently on the inside of the cover. Jeremiah 31:3 is a text often used by Jewish Christians to emphasize continuity with their ancestral faith.

Two songs on his next album, *Shot of Love* (1981), reveal the direction Dylan is heading. The first is "In the Summertime," where Dylan wonders about the spiritual rollercoaster he has been riding. "I was in your presence for an hour or so / Or was it a day? I truly don't know." His faith has turned into something more private and enduring, having gone through the fire of public derision. "And I'm still carrying the gift you gave / It's a part of me now, it's been cherished and saved." Framed by some of Dylan's best harmonica playing, the chorus sets a wistful mood: "In the summertime, when you were with me."

"In the Summertime" paves the way for "Every Grain of Sand," one of Dylan's many masterpieces. This song argues that the doctrine of Providence is the answer to the problems entailed in revivalism. We cannot always live in summer. Winter has a way of coming around whether we like it or not. America's greatest hymns were once inspired by the doctrine of Providence, but rock and roll typically celebrates the unbounded freedom of the individual. In this song, Dylan fuses rock and roll with Calvinism, bringing rock back to its deepest American roots. The first stanza sets the confessional tone:

> In the time of my confession, in the hour of my deepest need
> When the pool of tears beneath my feet flood every newborn seed
> There's a dyin' voice within me reaching out somewhere
> Toiling in the danger and in the morals of despair.

This song seems to be about the singer, but it is not. It is about gaining freedom from the self through trusting in God's administration of everything that happens to us. The image of Dylan's dying voice reaching out somewhere is potent, given the aging of his voice. The phrase "the morals of despair" is striking, because despair does have its own morality, even though it is a dangerous one. The second stanza spells out Dylan's realization that he must trust in God's plan:

> Don't have the inclination to look back on any mistake
> Like Cain, I now behold this chain of events that I must break
> In the fury of the moment I can see the Master's hand
> In every leaf that trembles, in every grain of sand.

The first two lines are in tension with each other. Dylan does not want to look back, yet he wants to break free from the chain of causality that keeps him in place. The futility of his fury convinces him that he must submit everything to God. Only by believing that God has made the past can we venture forth into the future with glad hearts.

Dylan needed to believe that history was on his side, because the public sure wasn't. Dylan has stated in interviews that the title cut of *Shot of Love* was his "most perfect song," that it defined him "spiritually, musically, romantically and whatever else."[21] Nonetheless, the album was dismissed by rock journalists as yet another theological sermon, and it was not commercially successful. Dylan has met many disappointments in his career, but this one probably led to some of his lackluster recording efforts through the late eighties and early nineties. In response to the poor reception of his Christian albums, Dylan appears to have tried to suppress his faith by retrieving a traditional blues sound, and it did not always work.

The doctrine of Providence is not a cheery belief system. When it does not work well, it is likely to lead not to passivity but to despair—or, better put, to a passivity born from despair. The idea that our lives are not our own can be disorienting as well as comforting. We can begin to lose hope that anything matters. It takes incredible faith to believe that everything happens for a reason that is absolutely hidden from our sight. Providence makes history meaningful, but it also increases the mystery of time, since meaning unfolds so slowly that all we are left with is hope and patience. While revivalism keeps the spirit up, Providence keeps it closer to the ground. The sacred is found in everyday details rather than in the highs of peak experiences, because God has designed it all.

Yet if Providence can give rise to despair, it is not the despair of secular existentialism. Existential despair is defiant and nervous, because it poses a challenge to the absurdity of a cold and empty universe. Providential despair arises when, after you turn everything over to God, you feel like you have nothing left. This is a despair peculiar to those who have experienced a spiritual awakening. To be touched by Christ, as happened to Dylan, is something so extraordinary that you can begin to doubt your senses. You can think it was all a dream and, as with all dreams, you can begin to doubt its reality once you have returned to the waking state. Remaining in such intensity is impossible, so a decline in the passion of faith is all but inevitable. But then you come to recognize that even your straying is part of the journey. You understand that wherever you go, God is with you, and whatever you do is part of God's plan. You realize that you cannot go back to the zeal of youthful enthusiasms, but you come to see that all is not lost, and that others have carried on the faith even when you have faltered.

Dylan has treated this kind of despair in many songs since the early eighties. Particular attention could be given to *Oh Mercy* (1989), which is one of his most cogent works, both musically and morally. It is authoritative, confident, and clear in its message of personal responsibility in a world gone terribly wrong. The album that most explicates the providential turn in his theology, however, is *Time Out of Mind* (1997). If the Puritans who founded America could be beamed into the twenty-first century and taught the rudiments of rock and roll, this is the sound they would produce.

Time Out of Mind is rock for the ages as well as music for the aged. As the first great rock-and-roll album for adults over 40, there is a good case for arguing that it is Dylan's most coherent full-length work. The album sounds like one long song with various permutations of the theme. This is an album of despair in the providential sense, of one who is coming to recognize that faith is a dream, but it is a real dream, because it has been dreamed by God. At times, this album evinces what can only be called theological panic, but Dylan's sense of inevitability keeps the mood calm.

Rather than theological panic, it is better to place this album in the longstanding tradition in Christianity called "negative theology." Negative theology is undergoing a revival among professional theologians, because it can be expressed in exquisite dialectical formulations geared to those with a penchant for terminological innovation. Actually, its counterintuitive claims can be simply stated. Negative theology declares that only by going through the darkness can one experience the light. Not knowing is a kind—indeed, the most special kind—of knowing. *Time Out of Mind* suggests negative theology because its most repeated phrase is "I don't know." Dylan is not saying that he does not know about God. He is saying that God does not speak through what we already know. God reveals the divine self in the darkness of the cross. God is not nice, happy, and cheerful in a flippant sort of way. God meets us where we are, which means that he lurks in the shadows, so we must dwell there too if we expect to be found by him. This album is spiritually challenging because it helps us toward God by pushing us over the edge of our ordinary boundaries of knowledge,

Time Out of Mind was a commercial success, but some of Dylan's most ardent fans did not like it because they thought the lyrics were too simple and direct. Dylan's subsequent album, *"Love and Theft"* (2001), is more sophisticated, surprising, varied, and spontaneous, but *Time Out of Mind* is meant to plow deeply a more limited terrain. Many of the lyrics are direct quotations from traditional American songs or allusions to other songs (and to poets like John Donne and Robert Burns), but that is part of the message of the work. Dylan is beyond trying to be original. Dylan uses cliché and repetition because that is the condition of despair. The prose is not supposed to be smart and complex. Despair is mundane and devastating. It would be a charade to give it elegant elaboration.

Nevertheless, Dylan demonstrates that he has not lost his cunning edge when he subverts liberal political pieties on this album. Reviews rarely mention this, perhaps because such subversion is not usually taken as a sign of sophistication. Notice, though, the way he playfully toys with political correctness by resurrecting the old-fashioned meaning of "gay" in the line "I'm strummin' on my gay guitar" (from "Standing in the Doorway"), how he toys with his reputation for womanizing in the exchange with the waitress in "Highlands" (especially when he thinks she has told him he looks like he doesn't read women authors, and he responds by naming Erica Jong), and, in the same song, how he acknowledges criticisms of his political apathy when he has someone ask him if he has registered to vote (he does not answer).

Some of the same fans who complained about the simplicity of the lyrics on this album criticized the sound of Dylan's voice for being overproduced, with too much echo. Daniel Lanois, who produced this album as well as *Oh Mercy*, explained that the distortion was intentional: "We treated the voice almost like a harmonica when you over-drive it through a small guitar amplifier."[22] The result is eerie, metallic, and almost impersonal, but this is appropriate given the message Dylan wants to communicate. He is ghostlike in this music, speaking about his own life from the perspective of one who is almost dead, and coming to the conclusion that someone else has been in control all along.

The opening song, "Love Sick," sets the mood with the line "I'm walking through streets that are dead." A guitar is picked in the background as if it were keeping time in a tick-tock manner. The entire album, in the wake of this song, sounds like a lonely walk down a dark street—perhaps a sleepwalk in which the singer does not know if he is awake, asleep, or dead. The singer is a pilgrim, but he is walking so far and for so long that he is no longer sure of his destination.

"Love Sick" announces the album's theme of loneliness, indecision, and sadness. "I'm sick of love but I'm in the thick of it / This kind of love I'm so sick of it." Dylan can neither go backward nor move forward. He cannot renounce who he is or accept his condition. One stanza gets at his ambivalence:

> Did I hear someone tell a lie?
> Did I hear someone's distant cry?
> I spoke like a child; you destroyed me with a smile
> While I was sleeping.

The words are suggestive and rich. Dylan the songwriter is admitting that he is unsure about himself. He does not know what he has heard. He is suspending his self-confidence—a daring gesture for a man known for the clarity of his vision.

The next song, "Dirt Road Blues," is in the traditional blues style, but it is muted and softened so as not to intrude on the album's ambience. Then comes "Standing in the Doorway," which is slow and meandering. "I'm walking through the summer nights," it begins, and you believe it. This song gives the first clue that the singer is talking about both divine and human love. Perhaps the two are inseparable, since both go through a similar pattern of ecstasy, disillusionment, and renewal. "Standing in the Doorway" has some of the same old themes of persecution and abandonment that Dylan has been expressing from the beginning of his career, but there is something different here. "There are things I could say but I don't / I know the mercy of God must be near." Dylan is holding back, not because he wants to protect himself but because he wants to protect God. He has been left standing alone "in the dark land of the sun" but "the ghost of our old love has not gone away." The last stanza repeats his conviction that there is "nothing to be gained by any explanation." This seems directed at his critics who constantly want to know why he became a Christian and to what extent he has remained one. There is no way to explain what he has been through without betraying it.

> I'll eat when I'm hungry, drink when I'm dry
> And live my life on the square
> And even if the flesh falls off of my face
> I know someone will be there to care.

His very silence has liberated him to trust that God is still good.

"Million Miles" continues the theme of distance and disenchantment. Songs of lament like this one are hard to sing without sounding self-absorbed and melodramatic, but Dylan manages to sustain sadness throughout all of these tracks without flinching or giving into mere sentiment. These first songs are good preparation for what comes next. "Tryin' to Get to Heaven" is one of the most moving songs Dylan has written. It is a follow-up to "Knockin' on Heaven's Door," but it speaks that theme with more gravity and a darker recognition of the finality of our mortality. "You broke a heart that loved you / Now you can seal up the book and not write anymore." Here Dylan is feeling let down by the author of the book of books, which is a despair greater than any that can be brought on by a broken love affair.

"'Til I Fell in Love with You" adds some positive energy to the album's flow. It is slightly but not disruptively optimistic. The guitars are a bit more upbeat, although the tone is still subdued. The point of the song is that love is a burden, not liberation. Dylan was doing fine before he fell in love. As Dylan once said about his conversion to Christianity, "I was doing fine. I had come a long way in just the year we were on the road [1978] . . . but a very close friend of mine mentioned a couple of things to me and one of them was Jesus."[23] This song denies that secular or sacred love is always born out of need. It is a commentary, in a way, on his conversion, when God changed his life for the worse as well as the better. Dylan paid a heavy career price for becoming a Christian, but he does not regret it.

One of the most explicit references to God is in this song. "Now I feel like I'm coming to the end of my way / But I know God is my shield and he won't lead me astray." Nick Train has written the most theologically attuned review of this album, but he finds this comment to be "the most inconsistent line on the whole album."[24] Quite the contrary, this line is consistent with the way Dylan reiterates that he is tired of "trying to explain." What is there to explain about hearing the call of Jesus? Some people will not believe you, others will berate you, and you will doubt yourself, but you have to trust that the past makes sense to God, even if it does not make sense to you. The doctrine of Providence fits this tiredness well because, rather than explaining the vicissitudes of history, it puts an end to all possible explanations by referring all meaning to the hidden ways of God.

The positive energy of "'Til I Fell in Love with You" is important, because it prepares us to plunge into one of the most despairing songs ever written. In "Not Dark Yet," the implicit religious theme of the album becomes explicit. Dylan sounds like he is letting go of the words through dying breaths. What makes it powerful is the "yet" in the refrain. Dylan's despair has not yet reached the crisis point, which makes it worse, in a way. If he had hit the cold darkness of rock bottom, he could begin the process of surfacing, but instead he is suspended in an encompassing grey. "I know it looks like I'm moving, but I'm standing still." This is music of the soul's winter. "I can't even remember what it was I came here to get away from / Don't even hear a murmur or prayer." If you listen too frequently and too closely to this song, you can begin to see depths of darkness that you hadn't imagined were so close by. Yet Dylan is not letting the darkness overcome him. He is right on the edge, looking down, but he is doing the looking for us, and so the song is holding us back.

The next song, "Cold Irons Bound," opens with some weird guitar reverberation, which makes you listen all the harder to the voice lurking in the shadows. When Dylan sings, in the first line, "I'm beginning to hear voices and there's no one around," you not only believe it but you feel it too. Dylan is singing on "bended knee," under "clouds of blood." He interjects a little humor when he pokes fun at the way his womanizing invades his churchgoing: "I went to church on Sunday and she passed by / My love for her is taking such a long time to die." A common Sunday school song that I grew up singing calls God's love "deep and wide," but Dylan confesses, "The walls of pride are high and wide / Can't see over to the other side." Pride is blocking his view of Jesus.

Dylan is providing the music for a spiritual appropriation of self-dissolution with lines such as "I'm waist deep, waist deep in the mist / It's almost like I don't exist." The title of "Cold Irons Bound" probably alludes to Psalm 107:10–11, which refers to those who "sit in darkness and in the shadow of death, being bound in affliction and iron; because they rebelled against the

words of God" (King James Version). The New Revised Standard Version is more direct: "Some sat in darkness and in gloom,
prisoners in misery and in irons." Dylan conveys the sense of
imprisonment and uses the imagery of chains throughout this
album. Many commentators on modern culture have talked
about how the corporate world leaves little room for the individual anymore. This is not Dylan's complaint. He is going deeper
than that. He is not saying that we need to be more individualis-
tic. He is saying just the opposite. We are imprisoned in our
individualism. We have become so opaque to ourselves that
our only hope is to bring the Western obsession with individualism to an end. The end of Western optimism, rationalism,
and individualism will be cataclysmic, no doubt, but Dylan is
giving us courage by both imagining and enduring that ending
in this song.

The negative theology of the self conceived by "Cold Irons
Bound" corresponds to a strong belief in the doctrine of Providence. Calvin, for example, so exalted God's sovereignty that he
did not think individuals were all that important in the scheme
of things. Calvin rarely talked about himself in personal terms
because he didn't think he was worth all the attention. He asked
to be buried in an anonymous grave so that his followers could
not turn his bones into relics. It is worth pausing here to underscore this point. The doctrine of Providence states that every
historical event is a manifestation of God's grace. The reason so
many Americans have turned their backs on this doctrine since
its heyday in the eighteenth century is that it tends to make pain
and suffering an integral part of God's plan. Americans tend to
be optimistic, so we treat suffering as something to be mastered
rather than something to be endured. We hesitate to attribute
the bad things that happen to us to a good God, yet Providence
asks us to imagine that God is most with us when we are most
alone. Darkness, after all, belongs to the light. In fact, darkness
is made possible by the light. Darkness shines with a truth that is

not its own, even as it threatens to nullify all truth in the depths of its emptiness.

The next song, "Make You Feel My Love," begins immediately with Dylan's voice, though the organ and piano are quick to join in. This song is a plea for love in the disguise of an offer to help. "I could offer you a warm embrace / To make you feel my love." This is the most hymn-like song on the album, but it also, on a first listen, appears to be the song most obviously focused on human rather than divine love. Dylan is asking for the opportunity to prove himself. The context is a failed pledge that can yet be redeemed. What signals the theology of the song is the desperation in his voice. When Dylan sings "You ain't seen nothing like me yet," we know it is bravado. He is insisting that he has not forgotten what it is like to love with one's whole heart. When heard as a plea for another chance, the song is haunting and heartbreaking. He knows that nobody can "make" anybody else feel his love, yet he wants to show that he still has love to give.

"Can't Wait" is not the strongest song on this album, though it does include a reminder that Dylan is still apocalyptic: "It's mighty funny, the end of the time has just begun / Oh honey, after all these years you're still the one." It combines his most characteristic theological conviction and his mastery of the love song in one couplet. Even this song, by continuing the acoustical coherence, sounds good, and would be a revelation if it were to show up on an album of lesser works. Its theme is bold. Dylan cannot wait any longer "for you to change your mind / It's late, I'm trying to walk the line." He is insisting on his vocation and his calling. He knows that he still belongs to God and wants God to give him the benefits of that knowledge.

"Highlands" ends the album on a note of hope. Of course, any song about heading toward the Scottish hillsides is going to raise the hope that we are treading a welcoming path. Critics are divided over whether the narrator is a fictional character or whether this song gets us into Dylan's head in a unique way. I think it is too confessional to be anything but the latter. Critics have also complained about the song's length, but each stanza is so concise that it has the feel of a journey on which you would not want to miss a step. Dylan's voice returns to the talking blues that he recorded early in his career. The theological overtones of the song are hard to miss. "Well my heart's in the Highlands whenever I roam / That's where I'll be when I get called home." He is waiting for "Big white clouds like chariots that swing down low." What is most remarkable about the song is the story he tells in the middle of it that at first seems nondescript to the point of irrelevance. It is a story about miscommunication, defeated expectations, and the impossibility of sharing loneliness. Dylan is saying, among other things, that even our most insignificant encounters are weighed down with meaning that we sense but cannot name. After his conversation with the waitress, he steps "back to the busy street but nobody's going anywhere." Every day is the same, he says, and he feels lost. He sees young people in the park, drinking and dancing. He crosses the street, "talking to myself in a monologue." By crossing the street, Dylan is admitting the allure of lost youth, but he is also saying that he realizes that there is more to life than trying to act like you are still a teenager. He is suggesting that the right to hope must be earned against the temptation of nostalgia.

> The sun is beginning to shine on me
> But it's not like the sun that used to be
> The party's over and there's less and less to say
> I got new eyes
> Everything looks far away.

This is the second to the last stanza, but the song should have ended here. The play on "sun" and its aural equivalent, "son," runs throughout the album, as when he sings, in "Standing in the Doorway," about the "dark night of the sun." This wordplay is brought to a profound theological conclusion by Dylan's admission that the sun now shines in a different way. The light Christ emits is a pervasive darkness that nonetheless changes the way we see. The last stanza ends on a more straightforward, positive note: "There's a way to get there and I'll figure it out somehow / But I'm already there in my mind / And that's good enough for now." That is too literal for the pain Dylan has evoked. The second to the last stanza says just enough to say it all. The sun is dark and the party is over. Dylan has new eyes, but what does he see? "Everything looks far away" could mean so many things. Perhaps the things that do not matter look far away, but perhaps the things that do matter look that way, too. When you get distance on the immature parts of your past, you get distance on the good things as well.

Time Out of Mind should have caused just as much stir as *Slow Train Coming*. This is the album where the train has arrived, but it looks pretty empty. Despair is just as much a part of faith as ecstasy and enthusiasm. Despair is the space within us that gives birth to faith, just as faith is the heart's long reach that makes that space look so bottomless and frightening. Despair of the kind Dylan dwells in is possible only for those whose faith is equally deep.

Blood on the Tracks is often called Dylan's most confessional and sorrowful work, but that album is mired in the predictable ups and downs of human love. On *Time Out of Mind*, Dylan is singing to his maker. He has gone beyond rock and roll and into the religious terrain of an original longing that makes all human affairs seem trivial by comparison. The result is transcendent, but it is also utterly human in its despair over experiencing a love that can never be properly returned. This is music of the Earth, where we always fall short, not heaven, where love will circulate in an economy of permanent surplus. The angels in heaven will probably sound a lot like Joan Baez (or better, the underappreciated Karen Carpenter), and the redeemed who will make up the joyous heavenly choirs will surely sound a lot like the backup singers on *Slow Train Coming*. Until we get to heaven, however, we will have to be content with a human voice, and there is none more human than Dylan's—and no album more expressive of the human condition than *Time Out of Mind*.

Notes

1. Teresa L. Reed, *The Holy Profane: Religion in Black Popular Music* (Lexington: University of Kentucky Press, 2003), p. 110.

2. See Avery Cardinal Dulles, "From Ratzinger to Benedict," *First Things* (February 2006), pp. 24–29.

3. Pope Benedict XVI (Joseph Cardinal Ratzinger), *The Spirit of the Liturgy*, trans. John Saward (San Francisco: Ignatius Press, 2000), p. 140.

4. Ibid., p. 146.

5. Joseph Cardinal Ratzinger, "Liturgy and Church Music," *Sacred Music* 112 (Winter 1985), p. 19.

6. Pope Benedict XVI, *The Spirit of the Liturgy*, p. 148.

7. The quotes are from p. 22 of the *Biograph* liner notes.

8. Beth Bailey, *Sex in the Heartland* (Cambridge: Harvard University Press, 1999).

9. Quoted in Heylin, *Behind the Shades Revisited*, pp. 719–20.

10. *Playboy* interview with Ron Rosenbaum, March 1978, reprinted in *Younger Than That Now*, p. 142.

11. Interview with Mick Brown, 1984, in *Younger Than That Now*, p. 190.

12. Interview with Neil Spencer, 1981, in *Younger Than That Now*, p. 182.

13. Ibid., p. 184.

14. Ibid., p. 156.

15. Wilfrid Mellers, *A Darker Shade of Pale: A Backdrop to Bob Dylan* (New York: Oxford University Press, 1985), p. 221. Also see Daniel Maoz, "Shekinah as Woman: Kabbalistic References in Dylan's *Infidels*," in *Call Me the Seeker: Listening to Religion in Popular Music*, ed. Michael J. Gilmour (New York: Continuum, 2005), pp. 3–16.

16. *Younger Than That Now*, p. 286.

17. See the important book *Christianity in Jewish Terms*, ed. Peter Ochs et al. (Boulder, CO: Westview Press, 2000).

18. For one of the more interesting examinations of Dylan's messianic Christianity, see the book by Ronnie Keohane, *Dylan & the Frucht: The Two Wits* (Fountain Valley, CA: Ornery Press, 2000). Keohane compares Dylan's lyrics to the writings of Jewish-Christian theologian Arnold Fruchtenbaum.

19. Quoted in Scott M. Marshall, with Marcia Ford, *Restless Pilgrim: The Spiritual Journey of Bob Dylan* (Lake Mary, FL: Relevant Books, 2002), p. 56.

20. Mellers, *A Darker Shade of Pale*, p. 213.

21. Quoted in Paul Williams, *Bob Dylan, Performing Artist, 1974–1986, The Middle Years* (New York: Omnibus Press, 1992), p. 202.

22. Quoted in Gray, *Song and Dance Man III: The Art of Bob Dylan*, p. 789.

23. Quoted in Heylin, *Behind the Shades Revisited*, p. 490.

24. Nick Train, "Cold Irons Bound—The Failure of the Sun," in *Bob Dylan Anthology Volume 2: 20 Years of Isis*, ed. Derek Barker (Surrey, England: Chrome Dreams, 2005), p. 295.

The Sound Wars
of Popular Culture

Christianity has a long history of expressing deep ambivalence toward the seductive power of music.[1] In the first few centuries of its growth, the church fathers decided to divide Greek culture in order to conquer it, adopting Greek philosophy, but rejecting Greek religion. This strategy shaped their understanding of music, which, to the Greeks, participated in both philosophy and religion. The church fathers shared the ancient Greek appreciation for the philosophical aspects of music. They admired the way music manifests mathematical relations. They also acknowledged that music provides unique access to the orderliness of nature as well as important insight into the mystery of how God harmonizes the apparent insignificance of humanity with the majesty of the cosmos. But the church fathers exercised strenuous restraint when it came to music's power of religious enchantment.

Following the precedent of the Old Testament, the church fathers were extremely suspicious of the frenzy that music could induce in some pagan rituals. Consequently, the church did not accept music as a direct channel to God, nor was its role in the liturgy ever thought to be so essential that it should supplant the spoken word. The relationship between music and math was blessed, but the association of music with dancing and math with numerology turned harmony, from the church's perspective, to sinful purposes. Numerical harmony could become dangerous when it was treated as a secret that could be pried open by bodily movement or speculative abstractions. Even where the relational complexity of music might have been most useful for Christianity, in plumbing the interpenetrating relationships within the Triune Godhead, theologians have been mostly silent.

The restrictions on music's range of meaning were lifted by the disestablishment of Christianity in the West. The privatization and marginalization of the church liberated the arts from ecclesial patronage and theological scrutiny. Nonetheless, music, of all the arts, has remained on the most intimate terms with religion. This liaison has been dangerous for Christian faith. The idea that music is sacred draws from the cultural endowment built up by the church, without reinvesting in the maintenance of the Christian tradition. Indeed, so many churches host musical events that it is becoming hard to tell the difference between a sanctuary and a concert hall. From the Romantics of the nineteenth century to the rockers of the twentieth, music has become the most serious candidate for a secular substitute for religion. It has done this by challenging the church for the right to be the primary carrier of humanity's deepest emotions. The Protestant Reformation began a turn toward subjectivity that urged men and women to discover the drama of life deep within their hearts. Music, it turns out, is, for many people, better at doing that than religion. Without religious formation, our hearts have little to say beyond their rhythmic beating. In an age when even the most devout believers know less and less about their theological traditions, music has the advantage of being a universal language that nonetheless relieves one of the obligation to speak.

Rousing hymns were essential to the success of the Protestant Reformation, just as rock and roll has been essential to the creation of the American teenager. It sounds curmudgeonly to complain about rock conquering the church when the churches that use rock are growing so fast. And it seems pointless to criticize a musical movement that is on the verge of conquering the world. Rock and roll is one of America's most successful cultural exports, the flip side of the evangelical style of Christianity that America has shipped to the farthest reaches of the globe. Rock and evangelical Christianity represent cultural aims that overlap in significant ways. Both use the latest technology to advance an agenda focused on individuals and their emotions. Both are suspicious of institutions and hierarchy. Both keep attention on the present by absorbing and taming every available style of personal expression. Both make listening easy, whether it is the sound of the sermon or the song.

Where rock and evangelicalism part company is less clear. They both make promises of pleasure, whether bodily or spiritual, that sidestep the need for discipline and tradition. Whether this difference makes any difference remains to be seen. One of the most pressing questions for the future of both religion and music is whether rock and evangelicalism will compete against each other for the global values market or collude in order to monopolize it.

Rock taken religiously and religion rocked are transforming the globe. Our senses have been musicalized, as George Steiner has pointed out in a number of books, and, I would add, our faith has been rock and rolled.[2] Much has been written about the growth of evangelical-style Christianity, but less attention has been given to the worldwide culture of rock and roll. Capitalism can be destructive of local cultures, so it makes sense that rock is its musical accompaniment. Throughout much of European history, music was lauded for its soothing properties. Rock and roll, rather than calming the savage beast, incites the complacent consumer. Rock says *buy*, just as evangelicalism says *believe*.

It is probably indeterminable whether rock is spreading across the globe in order to pave the way for capitalism or whether the spread of capitalism is paving the way for the triumph of rock. Some rock historians have suggested that the corporate takeover of rock means the end of anything like a rock culture. If this is true, then it is possible that what little cultural ambition rock has might be reborn in the church. Even the *New York Times* has recently discovered that Christian groups like MercyMe outsell the latest albums from Bruce Springsteen.[3] Is it too far-fetched to think that rock might find its voice by serving faith rather than fame and fortune?

Globalization might turn down the volume on rock as it morphs into world music, but it has spurred on the enthusiasm of the faithful. Christianity is growing, and southern hemisphere Christians are beginning to reverse the missionary process by bringing the good news back to the secularized north. This has not stopped left-leaning theologians from bemoaning the market pressures that are uniting the capitalists of the world. Open markets are the equivalent of the Roman roads that took Christian missionaries to what was then the known world. Christians can no more halt the processes of globalization than they can curb the insatiable demand for pop music.

Yet the Christian tradition can still speak truth about rock, and Bob Dylan's music provides a key to what the church should say. Many fans have noted how weary Dylan's voice has become as he has aged, as if he continues to sing in spite of himself. That weariness goes way back in his career. Dylan was never excited about cutting records, for example, and he was never eager to be a rock star. He always worked against the grain of his chosen profession. Dylan's ambivalence about popular music reached its apex in *Time Out of Mind*, which plugs rock into a message so somber that the mixture almost explodes. Christianity, too, I have argued, is ambivalent about the power of music. Dylan shows how this ambivalence need not necessarily mean the rejection of rock music. Rock at its best—given that Dylan is rock's best—can speak to our ambivalence about the promise and the dangers of musical rapture.

When Dylan went electric, he opened an audible gap between the generations. He also wrenched popular music away from the overly sincere leftist idealism of the folk revival. His voice resounded with the strains of the coming culture war. Music is still at the heart of battles over meaning and value, but the sonic landscape has shifted in unpredictable ways. As I wrote in *The Divine Voice*, a book that investigates the relationship between Christianity and the history of sound, rock has recapitulated the various forms of Christian theology in America: "The pietism of 1970s soft rock, the fundamentalist ranting of heavy metal, the sectarian primitivism of punk, the neo-traditionalism of orchestral rock, the spiritual elitism of the latest alternative music scene, the Pentecostal ecstasy of drug music, and the tolerant, liberal pluralism of world music."[4] Now that the lion of rock and roll has lain down with the lamb of Christianity, the old fault lines of theo-acoustical conflict need to be redrawn.

The latest sonic conflict to emerge on the cultural scene is the attempt to steer sound away from conflict altogether. Bookstore shelves are spilling over with texts about the healing properties of various tones, overtones, vibrations, and harmonies.[5] The New Age might be old hat, but never underestimate the power of capitalism to find fresh markets for old remedies that promise to comfort and soothe. Many of these books claim to rediscover ancient secrets about the relationships between mathematics, astrology, and harmonics. Others offer practical advice about how to meld your heartbeat to the pulsing rhythms of nature. Some hype medical miracles, while others offer a gateway to mystical ecstasy. The more spiritual examples of this genre typically draw from a medley of Eastern traditions, most prominently the Hindu system of energy centers in the body called *chakras*. When these books strive for seriousness, they often give some attention to the scientific study of sound, but all of them demonstrate the extent to which our hearing is historically constructed.[6]

What these breathless smorgasbords of soothing sounds have in common is a retreat from the era of rock and roll. Loud noise, after all, has been known to raise blood pressure and weaken the immune system. The Age of Aquarius was one of sonic exhibitionism, but the New Age is one of sonic insulation. The point of replacing electric guitars with Tibetan singing bowls is to soften your inner vibrations by synchronizing your moods with the rich simplicity of nature's harmonies. Focusing on a single hummed note and its overtones can quiet one's soul. In India, of course, these acoustical practices are rooted in a wide array of daily rituals and metaphysical beliefs. In America, they are abstracted out of that context and absorbed into a therapeutic milieu. Needless to say, the music merchants know how to turn the art of relaxation into a costly consumer affair.

Books on the healing properties of harmony demonstrate, paradoxically, a tremendous amount of pent-up anxiety in our society about sound. There is no doubt that urbanization and industrialization have led to a soundscape much noisier than anything our ancestors would have tolerated. The jacked-up decibels of modern clatter also means that we are losing our hearing at faster rates than people did in the past. Our greater toleration of loud noise has made rock and roll possible, and rock, in turn, is one of the causes of our diminished sensitivity to earsplitting sonic assaults. Sound is vibration carried to the ear by the medium of air, and rock goes out of its way to agitate and excite the vibrations it delivers. Rock is the form music takes when our skills of listening atrophy to the point where almost any noise sounds good. One reason we are such promiscuous hearers is that we are such indiscriminate lookers. That is, we are so easily distracted by the visual images that saturate our society that music must pound and boom to get our attention

One aspect of our current culture wars, then, is the conflict between the amplification and the simplification of sound, but this divide should not be exaggerated. Both rock anthems and New Age harmonies are intimately linked to the pleasures of the body. Both seek to instill a moment of ecstasy but, whereas rock does so most often in the shared experience of concerts, New Age harmonies help the lone individual to feel not so lonely. Rock arouses, while the tones of Eastern chanting pacify, but the endpoint of a self lost in sound is the same. Christianity, by contrast, is suspicious of sonic salvation not grounded in the spoken word. Conservatives of another era accused rock of guilt by association—due, that is, to its association with dancing and dancing's association with the breakdown of sexual barriers. New Age harmonies, meanwhile, are meant to remove whatever barriers exist between you and your body, so that you can be perfectly at ease with yourself. The spoken word, by contrast, especially in its liturgical consummation in Christian worship, draws the individual into a community of hearing that nonetheless preserves the sanctity of each individual life.

Phenomenologically construed, all music sways between the two poles of natural harmony and unnatural ecstasy. Music would be impossible if everyday life did not have its own rhythms, but music would not be so impossibly passionate if it did not offer to transport us out of the everyday and into another world altogether. What makes music truly profound is its promise that there can be a bridge between natural harmony and unnatural ecstasy. Music is that bridge, asking us to trust the tune as we make the connection between the order of nature and the disorder of our hearts. Mathematics is the most abstract and universal language of nature's laws, but music hints that those laws, instead of constraining us, can be the fount of our freedom. This too is what Christianity has insisted, over against every kind of paganism. God created the world in an orderly fashion so that we might be grounded as we reach for the stars. Theologically put, creation is not inherently at odds with salvation. Grace completes, rather than demolishes, nature. Heaven is Earth transformed, not Earth destroyed and replaced.

The gnostics of the early Christian era taught otherwise. They brazenly mixed pagan, Jewish, and Christian beliefs into a sophisticated but obscure theological system that took great liberty with the Christian faith. As might be expected, their imaginative approach to religion appealed only to the elite; in fact, they sneered at regular, everyday Christians who followed the consensus of church authority. Among modern scholars and others disenchanted with organized religion, their rejection of orthodox Christian faith has made them heroes of the ancient world. Secular liberals like to think of them as embattled and marginalized freedom fighters, but the truth is much more banal. Their metaphysical speculations had little widespread appeal. If the Christian church had not triumphed over them with such completeness that they were for all practical purposes lost to history, they would be significantly less celebrated today.

The gnostics argued that a lesser god, perhaps a demon, created the world, because this world is too deficient to be our home. Our souls, gnostics believed, are homeless until they escape this life for a better one above. This journey requires secret passwords and cosmological credentials, because the transition from the disorder below to the order above is precarious and full of danger. The Earth, then, is decidedly not harmonious, and ecstasy can be had only be diverting our attention away from all the chaos that imprisons us. By implication, music must be destructive—or at least seductive, by tricking our senses—before it can liberate. Traditional Christians rejected the gnostics because they accepted the goodness of the Earth. Christians believed then as they do today that God loves what he creates, and that he so loved this world that he entered into it as one of us.

When rock turns gnostic, it threatens to disrupt the precarious balance of harmony and ecstasy. Order and passion become polarized in rock's embrace of alienation and danger. This does not mean that all hard rock is gnostic, or that gnostic rock is always hard. The gnostic tendency in rock can perhaps best be heard in sentimental and idealistic songs about teen love. These songs reject this world for not being the kind of place where true love can be realized. They depict romance as a passion impossibly at odds with the constraints of everyday life, including the commitment of marital fidelity. Romantic love becomes a god who rewards reckless behavior with the momentary release of a drug-like high, but at the cost of steadfast attachments to the fragile relationships that bind us to the commonplace and the everyday. Gnostic rock says that only the unnatural is true; ecstasy must turn its back on harmony.

The heretical theology of Gnosticism provides the intellectual backing for rock culture by arguing that pleasure can be had only at the price of transgression. Gnostic rock performs a drama of excess that invites listeners to overstep their habitual limits. That is why so much rock is spectacular, in the sense of demanding our complete submission to its visual and auditory assault. Rock concerts use light to blind as well as noise to deafen. By deafening our ears, rather than tuning them to a heightening of the rhythms that surround and sustain us, gnostic rock denies the Christian truth that beauty is simple and truth is healing.

Dylan is the least gnostic of all rockers. In the liner notes for "Every Grain of Sand" in *Biograph*, Dylan devastates Gnosticism with an offhand comment: "That lie about everybody having their own truth inside of them has done a lot of damage and made people crazy." And he tells Cameron Crowe that when he listens to music, "I always like to think that there's a real person talking to me, just one voice, you know, that's all I can handle."[7] Gnostics listen to music to alter their perception of reality because they think reality is an impediment, rather than a sacrament, of divine love. Dylan wants to keep the music honest and real. He is a monotheist of sound. His music bridges harmony and ecstasy by heightening the revelatory power of the vocalized word.

One could argue, of course, that all music is gnostic in its promise of secret knowledge and its invitation to enter into a world where passion is unrestrained. Here some remarks from the much-neglected French philosopher Vladimir Jankélévitch (1903–85) are helpful. Jankélévitch has written movingly about what he calls "the state of exaggeration that music creates in its listeners."[8] By heightening the natural rhythms of life, music is the auditory equivalent of the rhetorical trope of hyperbole. As exaggeration, music does more than embellish; it transports the listener to a state that lies beyond truth and falsity. Truth is a property of words, but music, according to Jankélévitch, has nothing word-like to say. He even denies that we can speak about music with any cogency. Music, death, and God all frustrate our stammering attempts at explanation and show how even our most sophisticated discourses are little more than chatter. One might think *with* music, he says, but one does not think *about* music. At least, one cannot think about music with any kind of clarity or precision while one is listening to music. Jankélévitch would agree with George Steiner's comment, "Where we try to speak of music, to speak music, language has us, resentfully, by the throat."[9]

Music does not lie, it has been said, but then again, as Jankélévitch points out, it does not speak, either. But it moves, and of all music, rock moves the fastest. Fast and loud, rock quite literally silences audible speech. In a way, all music aspires to silence speech, but rock does that with a force that borders on violence. In its essence, Jankélévitch writes, "Music is the silence of words, just as poetry is the silence of prose."[10] Jankélévitch is intrigued by the moment of silence that immediately precedes the start of a concert, and he concludes that at its best music does not silence speech merely by its sheer sonic power. Instead, music speaks in and through silence, requiring listeners to be silent in order to hear anew. But what does music say if we cannot respond to it in words? Perhaps the most we can say is that it restores silence to us in a renewed and holy form. Paradoxically, it is only in listening to music that we can be truly quiet.

Dylan asks us not to listen to what he sings but to listen to how he hears. He is a great singer because he is a great hearer, not because he has an abundance of natural vocal talent. He hears his voice into being, and offers us the occasion to learn how to hear what the human voice means. But why is hearing so important to us? And why do voices have the power to command our assent? In listening to any voice, but especially his, we are prompted to hear the silence out of which speech comes, and if we are truly blessed, we can hear an echo of the first voice— God's Word—that, by speaking the world into being, gave us silence so that we might hear.

Notes

1. For a fine discussion of this ambivalence, see David Martin, *The Breaking of the Image: A Sociology of Christian Theory and Practice* (New York: St. Martin's Press, 1979), chap. 9.

2. See, for example, George Steiner, *In Bluebeard's Castle: Some Notes Toward the Redefinition of Culture* (New Haven: Yale University Press, 1971), pp. 115–24.

3. Kelefa Sanneh, "Christian Rock Is Edging toward the Mainstream," *New York Times*, April 27, 2006, B1 and B6.

4. Webb, *The Divine Voice*, p. 108.

5. The best of these books, many of which are really interesting, include the following: Mitchell L. Gaynor, *The Healing Power of Sound: Recovery from Life-Threatening Illness Using Sound, Voice and Music* (Boston: Shambhala, 2002); Kay Gardner, *Sounding the Inner Landscape* (Stonington, ME: Caduceus Publications, 1990); James D'Angelo, *Healing with the Voice: Creating Harmony through the Power of Sound* (Hammersmith: Thorsons, 2000); John Beaulieu, *Music and Sound in the Healing Arts* (Barrytown, NY: Station Hill Press, 1987); Joshua Leeds, *The Power of Sound: How to Manage Your Personal Soundscape for a Vital, Productive and Healthy Life* (Rochester, VT: Healing Arts Press, 2001); Shalila Sharamon and Bodo J. Baginski, *The Chakra Handbook* (Wilmot, WI: Lotus Light Publications, 1991); and Hans Cousto, *The Cosmic Octave: Origin of Harmony* (Mendocino, CA: LifeRhythm, 2000). Many of these books on the healing property of harmonics depict silence as the ultimate source of sound and thus the goal or endpoint of sound as well. From this perspective, sound exists in a sea of silence, breaking into our attention and spoiling our calm; complementary vibratory patterns can cancel out competing noises and ease us back into a peaceful oblivion. From a Christian perspective, silence exists as the refinement of listening, rather than its annulment. Silence is a cultural achievement that is accessible only to those who have learned to listen well, and it serves the function of heightening the uniqueness of vocalized speech.

6. I am not arguing that *all* hearing is socially constructed. Jonathan Sterne is a strict social constructionist, which leads him to argue that any attribution of essence, interiority, or naturalness to hearing is evidence of "religious prejudices." He is right, in a way. Without a metaphysics of sound, grounded in God's decision to speak the world into being and God's creation of humanity as hearers of the divine Word, sound has no essence and hearing no coherent history. What is puzzling is the ground on which Sterne can reject the religious interpretation of sound as mere prejudice when his own methodology limits his analysis to the telling of one among many possible histories of sound. His reading of the religious history of sound is an example of the very transhistorical gesture that his materialism calls into question. See Jonathan Sterne, *The Audible Past: Cultural Origins of Sound Reproduction* (Durham, NC: Duke University Press, 2003), pp. 14–19.

7. *Biograph*, p. 31.

8. Vladimir Jankélévitch, *Music and the Ineffable*, trans. Carolyn Abbate (Princeton: Princeton University Press, 2003), p. 98.

9. George Steiner, *Real Presences* (Chicago: University of Chicago Press, 1987), p. 197.

10. Jankélévitch, *Music and the Ineffable*, p. 139.